In ♥ sight

EMBRACING LIFE, DISCOVERING BEAUTY, GRACE AND TRUE PURPOSE

KATHLEEN WEBSTER-O'MALLEY

EMBRACING LIFE, DISCOVERING BEAUTY, GRACE AND TRUE PURPOSE

KATHLEEN WEBSTER O'MALLEY

All Rights Reserved

No part of this book may be reproduced or transmitted in any form or by any means, electronic or mechanical, including photocopying, recording, or by any information storage and retrieval system without written consent of the author except where permitted by law.

COPYRIGHT

Insight: Embracing Life, Discovering Beauty,
Grace and True Purpose

ISBN-13: 978-1-7356938-1-1
Copyright © 2020, Kathleen Webster O'Malley

omalley.kathleen@gmail.com
Worcester, Massachusettes
Copyright © 2020

Library of Congress in Publication Data
Webster O'Malley, Kathleen
Insight: Embracing Life, Discovering Beauty,
Grace and True Purpose
Copyright © 2020

Written by Kathleen Webster O'Malley
Edited by Kathleen Webster O'Malley
Book Cover Artwork by Raymundo Romero
Complete Book Cover Design by Zorina Exie J. Frey, IWA Publications
Interior Layout Design by Zorina Exie J. Frey, IWA Publications

The author of this book does not dispense medical advice or prescribe the use of any technique as a form of treatment for physical, emotional, or medical problems without the advice of a physician, either directly or indirectly. The intent of the author is only to offer information in a general nature to help in your quest for emotional and spiritual well-being. In the event you use any of the information in this book for yourself, which is your constitutional right, the author and the publisher assume no responsibility for your actions.

"Whatever resonates with your soul is truth…"

~Dr. Wayne W. Dyer

Written

in honor of my grandparents

Joseph M. Webster &

Virginia B. Harrigan~Webster

Dedicated to

Krista S.

& her family and friends

Contents

Author's Note..15

Introduction: Integrity, Intention and Purpose..............21

Chapter 1: **L**ifeward………....................Healing and Transcending Deep Sadness.....29

Chapter 2: **O**penness………….................Healing and Transcending Judgment............45

Chapter 3: **V**itality……….…..…...............Healing and Transcending Betrayal..............61

Chapter 4: **E**ssence……….....................Healing and Transcending Abandonment.....73

Chapter 5: **H**armony……..…................Healing and Transcending Envy....................83

Chapter 6: **O**neness……….................Healing and Transcending Non-Belonging...93

Chapter 7: **P**urpose……….....................Healing and Transcending Powerlessness....109

Chapter 8: **E**xpression………..................Healing and Transcending Self-Doubt.........121

Chapter 9: **G**enius............................Healing and Transcending Conformity......133

Chapter 10: **R**everence............................Healing and Transcending Worry...............143

Chapter 11: **A**lignment............................Healing and Transcending Displacement...153

Chapter 12: **C**reation............................Healing and Transcending "Original Sin"..165

Chapter 13: **E**nduring............................Healing and Transcending Unforgiveness..175

Chapter 14: **P**resence............................Healing and Transcending Regret...............187

Chapter 15: **E**ase............................Healing and Transcending Enslavement....195

Chapter 16: **A**bundance............................Healing and Transcending Unworthiness...203

Chapter 17: **C**ourage............................Healing and Transcending Indifference......213

Chapter 18: **E**mergence............................Healing and Transcending Disintegration...223

4 Simple Practices for Self-Healing......237

Acknowledgements................................241

Suggested Reading................................245

About the Author...................................253

Author's Note

*Life can only be understood backwards,
but it must be lived forwards."
~Soren Kierkegaard*

My legal name is now Kathleen O'Malley, *"a fine Irish name"* I've been told numerous times over the phone by persons who had no idea they were speaking to someone who was born and raised among three Caribbean islands of four differing nations. *You should name her Kathleen Jeannette*; a French nurse had said to my seventeen-year-old mother. Circumstances resulted in me spending my early years in the care of my maternal grandparents. From my grandmother, I adopted a deep respect for the earth and for the sea. My grandfather's gentle and affirming voice also became my affirming voice. In his arms, I would often fall asleep. My mom did resume care of me when I was approaching the age of five as there were teachings I needed to learn from my time with her and the man she had since married, who raised me as his own and became my father.

    From an early age I was a seeker, rarely without a journal or a book. I had dreams of becoming a writer but was encouraged to become a doctor by my seventh-grade math teacher who affirmed that I would be successful in my studies. Since the desire to heal others was within me, there was no resistance to pursuing a career in the field of medicine. I chose to enter the field of chiropractic instead of traditional medicine. What I did not realize back then is that I could also help others to heal through my written words.

I became a chiropractor at the age of twenty-six and left chiropractic school with not only a mission of helping others to heal, but also with my future husband. During this period, life seemed magical. This is how I determined I was on the right track. Everything worked beautifully. I chose to further my training in the care of women in pregnancy and to be a part of the creation of new life was amazing. I was certain I had found my calling and I soon began my own journey into motherhood.

Our first daughter was born prematurely, weighing four pounds, seven ounces. Although it was not the childbirth experience we had envisioned, we were still ecstatic. About two years later, we learned that we were expecting another baby girl. For unknown reasons, Jade Morgan was born extremely premature and her physical life ended shortly after birth. This was on June 10, 2006 and was the catalyst for my journey of self-discovery. I wanted to understand how this could have happened with all my efforts to nourish my body and my spirit. When asking *"why"* seemed to be in vain, other questions began to surface. *"Who am I, really? What am I truly meant to be doing with this life?"*

Then on January 1, 2010, I prematurely delivered our stillborn son, Jackson Thomas. Again, no explanation or known medical cause. In my daughter's words, "It's okay momma because now Jade isn't alone anymore. She and Jackson can play with each other in heaven and you have me." She was just five years old and I can clearly see why we are meant to have this physical time together. It was not until after the moment of her birth that I truly began to understand my capacity for love. She has also helped me to see the "dancing leaves" on a windy day, "a chocolate rainbow" after spilling my breakfast shake and the "Eiffel Tower" when you stick a white plastic fork into a square piece of cake. She continues to be one of my greatest spiritual teachers and a source of much inspiration.

My plan was to have two children, but Life had other plans. It seems that I was meant to nurture more than just my own children. Doors opened so I could be a voice of encouragement and inspiration for others. This entire journey has surely deepened me. My faith and belief in the goodness of life have seen me through. Looking back, I now understand and accept my journey—yes, all of it. It has taken much growth and healing to get to where I am.

You need to tell your story to at least one other person, a dear friend had said. I never imagined that I would be sharing about my experiences and my journal entries so openly. I would have much preferred to write solely fiction, but again, Life has had other plans.

I now see that the life within us can provide extraordinary guidance. In order to hear these whispers of our heart, we must first be open to receiving them. We must be willing to accept guidance, releasing our expectation of how this guidance will come. We must spend time in silence and befriend the stillness. It is in this sacred space that we begin to see more clearly that together we have everything we need in order to transcend our most challenging experiences and grow in love and compassion for ourselves and for each other.

The more I learned to let go, the more I was able to pay closer attention and notice whatever came my way. While attempting to declutter my desk one day, I came across our son's birth certificate. This was in October of 2011 as I was completing the writing of my first book, *Messages from Within*. It was then that I realized that not only was Jackson born on 1/1/10, but he was also delivered at 11:10 pm. Could this be the reason these numbers had been appearing all week long?

The numbers 111 and 1110 continue to appear before me on license plates, grocery store receipts, clocks, just about everywhere you can imagine. Whenever these numbers appear, I sense that Jackson and other guides are near; accompanying me in whatever decision or action is before me. This awareness fills me with peaceful contentment, realizing that I am not walking this earth alone.

Jade's sign to me has been butterflies. Yellow and black swallowtails showed up on the day of her burial (June 16, 2006), three times that day to be exact. They continue to come around when my thoughts are on her, reminding me that life is eternal, and love has no end. It seems that all my children have been instrumental to my journey of healing and awakening.

Still, it is not always easy to share openly about one's life. It takes courage to live openly and authentically and yet it brings about the greatest sense of freedom. When we allow our truth to be revealed, we begin to recognize our divine nature and see the pure miracle of our existence. This allows us to live with greater compassion and accept others as they are. We are woven into "a single garment of destiny" wrote the Reverend Dr. Martin Luther King, Jr. We each supply a thread.

So, live your truth. I trust that sharing the messages of my dreams and lived experiences might serve in awakening your soul's dream. Your soul's dream is who you truly are. And who you are is your greatest gift to humanity.

Kathleen Webster~O'Malley
June 20, 2020

Kathleen Webster O'Malley

Introduction

Integrity

Be honest in all aspects of your life. Seek to know who you are and who you desire to become.

In a region once known as the Gold Coast in West Africa, the Dagara people gather in celebration whenever they hear a woman has become pregnant. While in the mother's womb, shamans communicate with the life force of the fetus to discover why it is coming into the world at this time in history and what gifts it might hold for the village or community. Once the council of elders and the shamans identify the chosen purpose of this new life, the villagers are then charged with the responsibility of helping this child to remember what is often forgotten at the time of birth—*why am I a part of this life…in this place…at this time*? Once born, the invisible world of Spirit and the ever-present ancestors also inform and provide guidance through moments of inspiration, intuition and dreams.

For as long as I can remember, I have had vivid dreams. When

I was just a child, I dreamt I was walking on a beach one day and came upon a crib. Standing on the tips of my toes, I looked over the rail of the crib to see a fish inside. When I told my grandmother of this dream, she said it meant that someone was pregnant. *Oh, because of the crib*, I had thought. "No," she said. "Because of the fish." And as with most grandmothers, her wisdom proved to be true. A dream of fish has preceded every pregnancy I have ever had.

In recent years, I have become deeply aware that some things work together in ways far beyond what I alone could have imagined. A random thought turns out to be not so random. A series of dreams and synchronistic experiences, a car accident, a beloved teacher now in Spirit and a young woman who passed away unexpectedly in August 2011 were all integral to how this book you are now reading came about. Perhaps the Reverend Dr. Martin Luther King, Jr. *(January 15, 1928 ~ April 4, 1968)* said it best:

> **"We are caught in an inescapable network of mutuality, tied in a single garment of destiny. Whatever affects one directly, affects all indirectly. I can never be what I ought to be until you are what you ought to be. This is the interrelated structure of reality."**

Now, possibly more than ever, the world needs us to unearth our dharmic gifts for the fulfillment of a shared purpose. It is not enough to wait until our leaders figure it all out and determine what is best for the *greater good*. It is up to each of us to determine who we are and what we are meant to be doing for the betterment of our own lives, extending to our family, our neighborhood and our surrounding community. How do we begin this ever-evolving process of determining who we are?

To know ourselves fully is to transcend patterns of woundedness that have existed in our ancestral lineage and continue to exist in our biofield. We become fully ourselves when we transform self-doubt into discernment, powerlessness into a sense of purpose, and unrelenting anxiety into a deepening trust in the guidance that resides within and the guidance available from the unseen world. We become fully ourselves when we transcend labels and allow others that same freedom.

How this part of my journey began…

In August 2008, I was experiencing signs of another miscarriage. As I sat on the living room couch with my then four-year old daughter cuddled next to me, I turned on the television. I closed my eyes, with my head tilted back, expecting to hear one of the PBS shows that she found entertaining. Instead, I heard a man's voice saying exactly what I needed to hear in that moment. His message continued to provide much comfort as I did miscarry a few days after. These words were, "If you knew who walked beside you at all times, on this path that you have chosen, you could never experience fear or doubt again." This man was Dr. Wayne Dyer *(May 10, 1940 ~ August 30, 2015)* and this PBS program revolved around his book, *The Power of Intention.* From that day forward, Dr. Dyer's teachings have been a source of much inspiration. I had hoped to one day meet him in person and express my gratitude. However, the Source of all-that-is had other plans. I share more about this in Chapter 2.

Begin with Chapter 17 is the guidance I received in May 2017 before I had any idea what Chapter 17 would be about. Yet, I already had a working title, "In♥Spired," and an acrostic-style outline with the words,

L-O-V-E, H-O-P-E, G-R-A-C-E and P-E-A-C-E

This acrostic appeared to me on October 3, 2015, but unlike other inspired writing, it was not during my early morning meditation or while journaling. I was in the middle of folding laundry when I felt compelled to grab a sheet of paper. I felt guided to write **L**ove, **H**ope, **G**race and **P**eace vertically on the page and then began to record corresponding words that came to mind in quick succession—**L**ifeward, **O**penness, **V**itality, **E**ssence—**H**onor, **O**penness, **P**urpose, **E**xpression. When I wrote **G**enius for the G- in **G**race, I was certain that I was not the only one directing this. My G- word would have been Generosity or Gratitude. The title, *In♥Spired*, seemed appropriate since I felt as though Dr. Dyer might somehow be assisting me in this writing.

However, about three or four months later I learned that Hay House, Inc. would be releasing a book by Dr. Wayne Dyer titled, *Living an Inspired Life: Your Ultimate Calling*, a re-release of his previous title, "Inspiration." It seemed that the book I imagined I was being called to write had already been written by someone I greatly admired.

Over a year later, May 13, 2017, I was listening to a recording of Dr. Dyer as he spoke about *The Impersonal Life*, a book that was originally published anonymously in 1914. I heard Dr. Dyer say that this book written by Joseph Benner *(January 3, 1872 ~ September 24, 1938)* contained eighteen chapters, a commonality he noticed among sacred texts. As he began reading from Chapter 17 titled, *Finding Me*, I was reminded of the acrostic that had been tucked away in one of my journals. *Chapter 17* continued to echo in my mind as I searched for it. Once I found it, I decided to number the words. This is when I discovered that there were eighteen words. The seventeenth word, the C- in P-E-A-C-E…Chapter 17…was Courage.

Begin with courage was the message that continued to appear in various forms. One morning I photographed a license plate that contained CH17. Still, I had no idea what I could possibly say about courage that had not already been written. That sense of *not knowing* is often my cue to just begin, honor the process and allow it to unfold. Not knowing where to begin, I waited. Patience has not always been my strongest quality and yet months seemed to quickly pass. Then I heard of another Hay House release, *We Consciousness*, this one written by psychic medium, Karen Noe, who specifically received messages from Dr. Dyer for his family and for the world. It seemed that someone else had received a similar inspiration so again I became discouraged.

Intention

Be clear about what you most desire and take steps in the direction of your dreams.

Then on May 6, 2019, I awoke from a dream, followed two days later by a car accident. The synchronicities that followed again led to this outline. This time, there was greater certainty that I would heed my initial inspiration and share the message of this book. On August 1, 2019, in a shared silence with my friend, Gail Van Kleeck, author of *How You See Anything is How You See Everything*, I began writing about courage. Gail and I would sit together on Thursdays in her home beginning at noontime, writing for at least an hour and a half. By the end of August, not only had I completed Chapter 17, but I also had a much clearer understanding of Dr. Dyer's message that *words come through us, not from us.*

Recognizing the *power of intention*, here are my current intentions for this book, although I will allow for it to unfold. I imagine even what

I initially wrote about courage might transform as I am transformed throughout this continuing process.

My Intentions for this book...

- For readers to embrace the concept that the challenges we experience may not always be easily resolved or understood, but are complex opportunities that grow us forward, while still allowing us to choose the direction of our lives.
- For readers to learn a practical method of self-inquiry that honors our emotional resilience, while recognizing that we do not have to remain in patterns of woundedness that have continually been repeated in our lineage; instead, we can actively participate in our own healing.
- For readers to confidently follow their inner urgings, transforming self-doubt into discernment, hopelessness into inspired action, as we learn to accept that life is continually unfolding, no finite destination, just moments to come to know ourselves more, discover our connectedness and allow for the emergence of something beyond our own imagining.

Throughout this book you might notice that I share what mystic and spiritual teacher Joel Goldsmith *(March 10, 1892 ~ June 17, 1964)* referred to as "the parentheses of life, the illusory boundaries we call birth and death" whenever I first mention an ancestor. I do so not only because of my affinity for dates, but also to honor the presence of all those who came before us, who are still guiding, allowing us to exist as we are now.

Throughout this book, I share a practical approach to becoming more aware, observing, exploring and sorting through your bodily sensations, thoughts, emotions and dreams in a non-judgmental way. This process is based on the teachings of French educator, Andre Rochais *(March 16, 1921~June 20, 1990)*. In this practice, you do not focus on the details of a situation or the people involved; rather, it involves deepening the awareness of oneself. H*ow am I experiencing this circumstance? What is within my power to change? Who am I now, after all that I have lived?* It is to fully acknowledge your experience, process all that you feel without any blame or censorship, and allow healing to occur at its own pace, trusting that your inner wisdom knows the best path to your healing. I include excerpts from my own journals so that this method might be more experiential, rather than solely instructional. I also offer practices and healing affirmations that serve to continue the process of transformation.

Purpose

Be still and come to know that for which you were created.

When we transcend the wounds of the past, it is not to deny them. Rather, it is to explore and decipher the gifts that emerge alongside them, through them, in light of them. You have to determine which language works best for you. This is my offering, based on my lived experience. Yet, I do not propose to have all the answers to your experience.

What I now know to be true is as Danish philosopher and author, Soren Kierkegaard *(May 5, 1813 ~ November 11, 1855)* once said, "Life can only be understood backwards; but it must be lived forwards." There is no doubt that life is complex, creative, often messy and unpredictable. And yet somehow along the way, we meet exactly who we need to serve as our guides; some seen, others unseen, some known, and others unknown. These guides serve in our journey of remembering; remembering that we are all children of the earth and of the sea; remembering that we share the same ancestors, yours are mine and mine are yours; remembering that rituals are not intended to be *hard and fast* rules, but are the framework for developing a practice, honoring all that we are, as we seek to become all we were intended to be; remembering that while we were chosen for this incredible journey, there are still choices to be made. Please accept this humble invitation to journey with me.

May the Source of light, love, hope, grace and peace guide our way.

Chapter 1

Lifeward

Just as a rose unfurls to greet the rising sun, what gives us life is also what sustains life. At our core, we are life seeking wholeness, love seeking connection, hope in search of greater fulfillment, joy, a sense of calm and peace, communion with Source, this Earth and with each other. Life inspires life. It embraces safety and comfort as well as adventure and more aliveness. It seeks newness and greater possibility. Life is creative and ever-changing, constantly expanding and becoming. Life is ever-present. All-that-is, has always been and forever will be.

Krista...

I never knew Krista, nor did I have a personal connection with any member of her family prior to August 2011. A social media post by a mutual friend shared the heart-breaking news that another young life had tragically ended. There had been an incredible outpouring of love for this young woman. From the comments, I gathered she was a generous soul with a larger than life personality, known for her smile, quick to offer a kind word and sparked much laughter with her sense of humor.

Larger-than-life is how many of these young souls are often described—Fun, loving, compassionate sons and daughters, sisters and brothers filled with such promise. Unexpected loss leaves behind many questions that are never fully explored out of respect for the grieving family. These questions are not intended to judge or be intrusive, but rather to shed light on what has become an epidemic. The American Foundation for Suicide Prevention (AFSP) released data from the Centers for Disease Control (CDC) on January 30,2020 which indicated that in less than two decades, the rate of suicide has increased by forty percent. Globally, according to the World Health Organization (WHO), one person is lost to suicide every…forty…seconds.

There are no chance encounters

I was scheduled to speak at a local library about my book, *Messages from within: Finding Meaning in Your Life Experiences* in March 2012. I had planned to talk about the "loneliness" of pain and how this young woman, although unknown to me personally, had somehow provided greater insight into my own tendency to hide behind a smile while carrying much hurt inside. The reality is that many of us keep painful circumstances and personal challenges well hidden. We manage to smile when someone makes a comment such as, "Wow, you look like you've lost twenty pounds," choosing not to mention that the apparent weight loss was a second trimester pregnancy loss. How did we become so adept at minimizing and repressing our feelings surrounding loss and other traumatic experiences? Many of us would rather isolate ourselves, becoming a homebody or recluse, rather than have conversations that

Love

reveal our vulnerability or risk causing others to feel uncomfortable.

And not only do we conceal our invisible wounds, but we also tend to hide our truest essence, some of our greatest gifts and deeply held beliefs for fear of judgment and criticism. When will we realize that true and meaningful connection does not equate with conformity? We do not all share the same origin, genetic expression, history or upbringing so naturally we are going to have varied beliefs and values. Even siblings or twins can experience the world differently with their distinct traits, patterns and gifts. Likewise, we all have varying mystical and spiritual dimensions which allow us to perceive differing degrees of reality.

My hope for that book event was to encourage others to take the time to explore their inner world and connect with others. What I did not expect is that Krista's mother would show up at my presentation that evening. We were introduced moments before I was to begin, and I immediately knew she was Krista's mom. For a moment I considered discussing a different theme from my book, but something within me said to just ask if she would be okay with me sharing about her daughter's impact on me. She was gracious in allowing me to do so.

About a week later, I received a beautifully handwritten note from another family member expressing her gratitude. That evening had been meaningful to her mom and provided some needed comfort. She went on to share other similarities between her sister and me. I was deeply touched by this note and desired to do more to provide guidance and emotional support to those struggling to find meaning and a sense of purpose in their lives. I did an internet search on suicide prevention and came across the *Samaritans*, known as a befriending group whose mission is *to alleviate despair, prevent isolation and reduce the risk of suicide.*

I arranged a meeting to learn more about volunteer opportunities with this organization. A few days prior, I was driving through the town of Framingham. I had been contemplating whether my already full schedule would allow for yet another commitment. Precisely at that moment, the traffic was slowing, and I looked to my right. Alongside the road was a sign that read, *Call the Samaritans, Volunteers Needed.* I had traveled this road many times before and not once had I ever noticed this sign. The message seemed clear and so I kept the meeting. However, as I sat with the director of the call center to learn more about their program, it became obvious that I would not be able to commit to the hours that I would be most needed. *So why was I led here,* I wondered.

Being guided from within

We are often moved to help in any way possible when tragedy occurs. It is one of our basic instincts and one of the most beautiful aspects of humanity—to extend kindness, provide respite and comfort to another being. It is equally as important that we honor all aspects of ourselves in order to be truly led to where we can best serve. I wanted to find a way to continue to honor Krista, but if I had chosen to override my inner signals and do whatever necessary to make this opportunity work, it would not have been sustainable long-term.

When we are called to something, it does not have to overextend our resources or negatively impact our wellbeing. A true calling enables us to use the best of ourselves and our greatest strengths. Rather than overextend, a true calling provides an abundance of resources. There is a sense of alignment; a feeling of where I am is where I am meant to be. While it may require effort, there is still a feeling of being at ease. The persons we love and care about would not want us to sacrifice our wellbeing in their honor. We honor them as we honor ourselves. This book is dedicated to Krista, her family and friends. The light within me burns brighter in part because she existed.

A few months after my meeting at the *Samaritans*, another opportunity presented itself. A dear friend and I were allowed to facilitate a group for young women ages sixteen to twenty-four. These incredible women from diverse backgrounds had experienced various challenges in their earlier lives. Our focus was on healing and growth. By creating an environment of respect, trust and encouragement, many of them eagerly shared about their present lives, their history, and their dreams for their future. Each Monday morning was an occasion to connect with these young people. Most mornings, I listened more than I spoke.

These were incredible poets and songwriters, talented singers and storytellers disguised as teens and young adults with a troubled past. And they all have a similar aspiration, to help others in the areas where they experienced the most pain. A young woman who experienced homelessness from age eight to eighteen desires to work with the homeless population, particularly children; Another who struggled with childhood illness dreams of becoming a pediatric nurse; A young mother who conceived a baby as a result of a sexual assault aspires to not only give this child an abundance of love and the best opportunities in life, but also wishes to pursue a career as a social worker. Their stories of resilience touched us deeply.

We are not meant to journey alone

We were often amazed at how easily these young women were able to share about their experiences, their family influences, their unhealed wounds, their aspirations. Hearing each other's stories allowed for a deeper understanding of one another. There is something powerfully transformative that happens when a person realizes that everyone has their share of challenges and traumatic experiences. It creates a type of kinship, recognizing that you are not alone, that you were not simply the unlucky one, that you are not damaged and not a perpetual victim.

It is also imperative that we recognize that healing in any form rarely happens alone. As one of my mentors, a Franciscan Sister would say, "We are often wounded in relationship, so we must heal in relationship." It is only through our connections that we come to know our true selves, our capacity for love and our capacity for healing. Healing does not always equate with finding a cure, but it paves the way for growth and transformation, allowing us to live more authentically amidst whatever challenge we are facing.

Transcending Deep Sadness

We experience pain and loss as part of this human experience. We must live through the difficult days as best we can. Some days are easier than others. The problem lies with the expectation to quickly *get back to normal. Don't dwell on what happened,* we sometimes hear. *Focus on being happy.* Feeling as though no one understands only deepens the sadness. The gravity of loneliness often leads to a state of hopelessness. There is no way to simply forget about pain unless we bury it under busyness and other compulsive behaviors. We might succeed at pretending it is not there and then like a dormant volcano, it erupts.

Many of us never receive the tools necessary to process and integrate life's challenges. We are not guided to reflect on our own intimate experiences and arrive at our own conclusions. Instead, we are constantly learning about the world from the perspective of others. We are taught who and what to be afraid of. We are taught what determines success and what constitutes failure. We are taught the mechanics of how things work and how to research other people's findings and arrive at a similar or expected outcome. We are taught which feelings are acceptable and how to avoid ridicule. We tend to focus on the usual and customary meanings of words and phrases without fully exploring how that word or phrase is received and felt within us. Language should serve in helping us to relate well to each other, rather than creating beliefs by which we judge one another.

There is more to learn

It might serve us well to learn how to decode our inner sense of restlessness rather than deny it. That uneasiness that comes with self-doubt often has more to say if we tune in and listen. That dissatisfaction we feel toward the current state of events might be a call to something greater. *What is this tension in my body? What underlies this reaction to a comment made by a stranger I will never encounter in person? How am I to live this situation better? What message does this dream hold for me? What is underlying this need to write? Am I being called to something more?*

This method of self-inquiry is based on my study and understanding of PRH (Personality and Human Relationships). It originated in France by educator and priest, Andre Rochais as a means of personal and spiritual transformation. It is based on the concept that we are always in the process of becoming *more*, not from a place of lack or deficiency, but *more* as in recognizing our unlimited potential. By answering targeted questions, we receive deeper insights about the varying aspects of ourselves. Once we recognize and understand our underlying needs, our ways of functioning along with our deepest motivations, we can then take responsibility and choose how to live our lives with greater meaning and purpose. We emerge with more clarity, a freeing, something that allows us to live with greater ease.

I wrote the following in my journal on the final day of a PRH workshop titled, *"Who am I?"*

> *April 6, 2008…Initially, I was anxious about sharing my innermost thoughts and feelings with complete strangers but was then surprised with the ease in which I was able to do so. With each written exercise, I was able to dig deeper within. I recall in the first weekend session, as I visualized my talents and gifts, I saw them at the bottom of a rocky chasm. Now, it is as though they are effortlessly floating upwards and becoming more tangible…*

Transcending deep sadness is about recognizing that everything we face is always leading us to uncover more of who we are and how we relate to the greater wholeness that exists. *Life might seem unjust, but what within me desires fairness and justice? How can I treat myself more fairly, with greater self-compassion? How can I then provide fairness and justice to another person? Life might seem hopeless, but what is at the core of my unmet needs or constant longings? How am I meant to heal and transform and possibly be a source of hope for others?*

It is important to keep in mind that we are infinite, always in-process, never reaching a fixed state or a static place. It is when we try to have it all figured out that we can easily become ungrounded. *There is more to learn* a teacher once said to me in a dream. This was soon after writing my first book, *Messages from Within*. I knew then I did not have all the answers, but I thought I had at least uncovered how I was meant to exist in this world. Sure enough, there is always more to learn.

Acknowledging the experience

Transcending despondency begins with a decision to move towards healing. We must first acknowledge our hurts and our longings in order to begin this process. Physical pain and/or emotional unease are often what signal us to take a closer look. And then there are times when you have no idea what happened. One day, life is as usual, well-sorted and stable, and then the next day you have no idea why you find yourself thinking about something that occurred years ago. *Why has this only now surfaced? Now what?* This might be the perfect time to heal from a past hurt because you now have the necessary tools, the needed support and a wider perspective in order to reclaim the essential parts of yourself.

There is a meme about letting go of the past that reads, *"Why look back, you don't live there anymore."* However, we can never ignore or deny what has shaped so much of who we have become. We sometimes revisit the past to see more clearly how our world has unfolded. We look back in order to understand the significance of our heritage and earlier relationships and to discover the patterns that have been repeated. We can look to our past and still choose healing for ourselves. We can choose not to repeat patterns that limit our full potential. We can look back and see how far we have come.

Acknowledging the experience: January 13, 2010…*Today is a real struggle. The pain I'm feeling is heartbreak…a sensation all too familiar, but no easier. Right now, I do wish there could be a fast-forward button that I could push and be transposed beyond this intense pain. I'm finding it difficult to focus on what-is rather than what could have been. I'm doing the best I can to be patient and take each day as it comes. It's really hard to do. I did not expect to be in this place again. It seems so unfair…*

Practicing self-compassion

Self-compassion requires practice as each day can arrive with its own set of emotions. Be respectful of your feelings as you write whatever comes to mind. Do not dismiss or discount anything. The great thing about journals is that they do not judge you or tell you how not to feel. Still, do not be harshly critical of yourself. *Brutal honesty is still brutal*, as a friend of mine would say. We can acknowledge the pain and disappointment without being overly critical of ourselves. As Louise Hay (*October 8, 1926 ~ August 30, 2017*) would tell us, "…criticism locks us into the very pattern we are trying to change. Understanding and being gentle with ourselves helps us to move out of it." We can state what we observe to be true in this moment and allow for other truths to emerge.

Self-compassion is not the same as being complacent. Instead, it recognizes that everyone heals at their own pace. Allow yourself adequate space and time to sort through your emotions. Reach out for support if you feel no forward movement. Hear what others have to say, but do not disregard your inner barometer. Listen for your innermost voice. It speaks with compassion.

Processing the emotions

Reflective journal writing, as taught in PRH is the process of connecting with your innermost Being, a non-physical aspect that holds your truest identity, your gifts and your deepest purpose. The Being is a place of richness and inner wisdom that can be accessed by first locating a felt sensation within the body. *What underlies this tension in my shoulders? What is this heaviness in my solar plexus? What is this frustration all about? Where is this self-doubt originating?*

Whether it is a sharp pain, mild discomfort, intense emotion, subtle uneasiness or tinge of excitement, you pay specific attention to whatever is felt, physically or emotionally. You do not consciously attempt to attach it to a past or present experience. You are not seeking a solution or one complete answer. Instead, you wait patiently to see what arises. You allow the sensation to lead you as you take time to get in touch with whatever this process is awakening in you. You explore with as much detail, keeping the focus on yourself, no blaming, no shaming, allowing yourself to be led deeper and deeper. Be patient. This takes practice.

Processing the emotions: January 15, 2010...*This emptiness I feel. It feels like an ache in my heart and uneasiness in my belly. In this moment, there is a sense of helplessness, a sense of powerlessness. I find myself holding my breath. Breathe...I make the effort to breathe more deeply, deeper into the emptiness, deeper into the helplessness, deeper into the powerlessness. I breathe...I allow the tears to flow as I breathe...*

A pen and paper have always been my preferred medium, while others might prefer the keyboard or sharing their thoughts aloud. For some, it is playing an instrument, painting, going for a walk or a run, fishing, or a mind-body technique such as Emotional Freedom Technique also known as tapping that allows for this processing to occur. The idea is to connect with your bodily sensations, feel whatever you feel and become aware of your deeper conscience and innermost wisdom. *What is your preferred way of processing your emotions? How do you move the energy through your body?* If you try one approach and it does not resonate, choose another.

What does my body need today?

The body is self-healing and self-regenerating once we determine what it needs and how best to nurture it. There is never a one-size-fits-all approach with healing. Our needs can be vastly different. I used to believe that once something was healed, it was forever done and over with. This certainly has not been the case. It seems that healing occurs in layers. To heal everything at once would overwhelm the body and psyche.

It is helpful to develop a daily practice of being fully present to ourselves by asking, *what do I need today? What would allow me to be at my best?* In an insightful poem written by Hollie Holden, she shares her body's answer, *"Could you just love me like this?"* There are times when this is exactly what our body needs, nothing more.

Find or create a healing circle

While we benefit from moments of solitude and stillness, we also need others to help facilitate our growth and healing. In addition to journaling and professional guidance, we benefit from healing circles—circles of women, circles of men and circles of men and women. We need groups that serve as a safe place, built on mutual respect, where we are allowed the freedom to express ourselves fully and where we can also accompany others in their continued growth and healing. In the midst of a circle, that which is sacred becomes even more visible. Burdens become easier to bear when we give and receive from the depths of our hearts.

~ PRACTICE ~

Moving Stored Energy through the Body

The intent of this practice is to dissolve and release the emotional charge that is often stored in the cells and tissues of the body. My practice involves first writing, drawing or painting my feelings. I tend to preserve most of my journals, but there are times when I use a fire ritual to burn what I have written or the pictures I have drawn, not with the energy of destruction but with the energy of release and surrender.

You can simply light a candle to honor the sacredness of your writing or painting or as you play an instrument. This is what my process looks like:

Observe: I observe my body, recognizing my connection to the ground and to this chair. I scan upwards from the soles of my feet to the crown of my head and back to my shoulders. I intend for any stored or trapped energy to surface gently, causing no harm as it makes it way upward, then downward, travelling into my arms, into my fingertips, through my pen and unto the page.

Write: I write, allowing any tearfulness that might arise throughout this process. I pause when necessary. I remind myself to breathe. I continue this process until the intensity of emotion diminishes. I sit awhile, giving space to anything else that might surface. When the process feels complete, I shift my attention to the flame.

Observe: I watch as the flame dances—as though the energy released from my body is being absorbed. I do this until the process feels complete. I then extinguish the flame and watch as the smoke travels upwards and dissipates. I imagine that energy being transformed into nothingness.

Allow space for healing thoughts

I take note of anything that arises during or after this process. I pay attention to any new sensations. I record any new insights.

The voice within says,

I am a creative being, constantly expanding and becoming. I seek to understand that storms naturally come and go, not to discourage or be destructive, rather, to alter the course when necessary. I choose to grow in love and trust the ever-changing voyage of healing and becoming free. I allow myself to steer towards all that gives and sustains life. I am life. I am love. I am...

Insight: Embracing Life, Discovering Beauty, Grace and True Purpose

Chapter 2

Openness

I awoke from a dream of Dr. Wayne Dyer on April 27, 2014. This was a Sunday. It was the second Sunday of Easter. That morning, I attended a service at St. Andrew's, an Episcopal Church once located in the town of North Grafton. How I came to be at this church seven years prior was through a spontaneous conversation in the floral section of a grocery store with a woman I would never see again. This woman had been a long-time member of St. Andrew's, but had fallen ill and entered a long-term care facility within a week of our conversation. That grocery store does not exist in our neighborhood anymore. It is as though everything that allowed this moment to be is no longer.

This particular Sunday, we were seated around tables as opposed to church pews for this special service. One of the women at my table shared about a reading from a spiritual publication known as *Forward Day by Day*. The message was about *seeing what we believe* rather than the popular phrase, *I'll believe it when I see it*. I had heard Wayne Dyer speak of this before, so this immediately called my dream to mind.

> April 27, 2014...*I see myself kneeling at the altar. This day, Dr. Dyer is our Eucharistic Minister. He is the one to place the communion wafer symbolizing the body of Christ into the palms of my hands. As he leans forward, he whispers, "See me after." The service comes to an end. I search everywhere. I cannot find him anywhere.*

A few days after, while attempting to declutter my desk, I came across a wellness magazine from six years earlier, March 2008. On the back cover it read, "There are those who say seeing is believing, I am telling you believing is seeing." This quote is attributed to Neale Donald Walsch. I share a photo of this issue of *Pathways* magazine in a blog titled, *Seeing the Perfection of the Universe in an Imperfect World.* The front cover appropriately reads "Gift from the future." The same message in two days caused me to take notice. What about the message *"See me after?"*

Seeing...

The day I learned of Wayne Dyer's passing, I had awakened with thoughts of him, but could not recall the details of my dreams that morning, which is unusual for me. Later that afternoon, I was at a neighborhood gathering where I ended up sharing this story of the "Cracked Pot."

> *A legend tells of a man who carried water from a stream to his village every day in two large pots tied to the ends of a wooden pole, which he balanced across*

his shoulders.

One of the pots had a crack in it, and while the other pot was perfect and always delivered a full portion of water at the end of the long walk, the cracked pot arrived at the man's house only half full.

Of course, the perfect pot was proud of its accomplishments, living up to the expectation for which it was made. But the cracked pot was ashamed of its imperfection, accomplishing only half of what it had been made to do.

After two years of what it perceived to be a bitter failure, it spoke to the man one day by the stream. "I am ashamed of myself, and I want to apologize to you."

"Why?" asked the man. "What are you ashamed of?"

"I have been able, for these past two years, to deliver only half my load and quench half of the thirst which awaits you at your home because this crack in my side causes water to leak out all the way back to your house."

The man smiled, and said, "When we go

back, be sure to take a careful look at the path along the way."

For the first time, the pot noticed many flowers and plants growing along one side of the path.

"Do you see how much more beautiful nature is on your side of the road?" commented the man. "I knew you were cracked and decided to make use of this fact. I planted flowers and vegetables, and you have always watered them.

I have picked many flowers to decorate my house. I have fed my children with lettuce, cabbage and onions.

If you were not as you are, how could I have done that?"

This story became a topic of conversation because when I first shared it in a social media post (July 18, 2015), to my surprise, the following day I noticed a clay pot in a neighbor's garden that had an obvious crack on one side. I cannot tell you the amount of times I have walked past this garden and not once before noticed this pot. I took a photo that morning and posted the image with a message that read, "Your mind is a garden, your thoughts are like seeds." Like seeds, our thoughts take root and grow. We tend to see more of what we focus on.

My neighbor, the owner of the cracked pot, was at this

Love

neighborhood gathering (August 30, 2015) and so I asked her what happened to the clay pot that used to be in her garden because I noticed it was no longer there. She explained that she frequently moved things in her garden, so she was unsure where she last moved it to. Within minutes of leaving this gathering, on my walk home, I received a notification on my phone from Dr. Wayne Dyer's Facebook page. This is how and when I learned of his sudden passing.

Be still …

The following day, midday, I was sitting on my deck, thanking Dr. Dyer for all his teachings. *What would you have me know*, I inquired with my thoughts. Just then, a Great Blue Heron flew by and landed in the pond to the left of me. I asked again, this time with my eyes closed. *What would you have me know*? And through the stillness I could almost hear him say, "*Come, let's take a walk. I'll show you.*" With my best bud at the time, a yellow Lab named Logan *(April 2006 ~ June 30, 2018)* who came to us in June 2007, I set out on a mid-day walk, wondering what Dr. Dyer would possibly show me. And there it was.

There in my neighbor's garden was the cracked pot, but it was not where I had originally seen it. It was on the other side of a shrub. I spotted it when Logan began sniffing around the area and instead of redirecting him, I followed. I couldn't help but think, *could this be what you wanted me to see, Dr. Dyer—that you are just on the other side?*

Believing I had seen what I needed to see, I headed back home. I was just about to go inside when I looked over to the pond. In that moment, the Blue Heron lifted out of the water and took flight. It was the most awe-inspiring sight. The gracefulness of such a bird with its long legs and enormous wingspan instilled such an incredible sense of peacefulness within me. While I wished I could have had my phone or other camera to capture this moment, I knew I was meant to experience it as I did, not through any other lens. *Thank you for this gift, Dr. Dyer.*

My attempt to share my experience of the Blue Heron with my husband was not met with the same level of enthusiasm. He responded with, "I see those birds on the pond all the time." So how did I not notice the presence of such a majestic bird before? Since then, whenever I am contemplating the direction of my writing, it seems that I encounter a Great Blue Heron. I imagine it to be a message from Dr. Dyer indicating I am in alignment with my call to write. Most recently (September 13, 2019) within days of listening to Wayne Dyer's 1990 recording of *You'll See it When You Believe it*, I came upon a Great Blue Heron. There it was standing, looking out at the water in the very spot I stood most mornings at sunrise. I had chosen a different route home that day because my daughter wanted to practice driving. I had her stop so I could take a photo. I share about this in a blog titled, *Seeing the Perfection of the Universe in an Imperfect World*. Less than a week later (September 19, 2019), I decided to register for a Hay House Writer's Online Course with the clear intention of continuing this writing and submitting a book proposal.

Synchronicity...

I did not always have an affinity for dates. As I share in my author's note at the beginning of this writing this came about after the birth of our stillborn son, Jackson Thomas (January 1, 2010). I was once told that this was a coping mechanism to help deal with all the loss I have experienced. *You look at the clock multiple times a day, and you see 11:08 and 11:09 just as frequently as you might see 11:10.* While this might be true, I also notice the moments that cause me to notice the time. For example, the ding that alerts me to low fuel at the exact moment my odometer reads 44 degrees, as I am traveling 44 miles per hour and it is 11:10 and on the dashboard, my temperature dial is set to high so what I see is, 11:10 Hi. I prefer my interpretation. It makes me smile.

Through journaling and revisiting old journals, I have come to notice how certain dates also repeatedly hold significance. For me, April 10th is one such date. On April 10, 1987 at the age of 13, I was travelling to the island of St. Croix for a much-anticipated spelling bee competition. April 10, 1999 was the eve of my graduation from chiropractic school. It was at an awards ceremony held on this evening that I received an offer for a significant job opportunity. April 10, 2011 was my first attempt at pregnancy through gestational surrogacy. And it was on April 10, 2013 that my husband and I came to the difficult decision to not attempt another embryo transfer as previously planned.

October 3rd is another significant date. I mention in my introduction how the outline for this book first appeared as an acrostic on October 3, 2015. Well, just earlier today (January 12, 2020), I was flipping through my second book, *Messages from Children and What They Can Teach Grown-Ups* and opened to the message titled, *Write it Down*, about the importance of giving shape and form to our innermost dreams and desires by placing our thoughts onto paper. In my earliest journal, I had written down my intention to one day write a book. I was fifteen. That date was October 3, 1989.

Transcending Judgment

While everyone wants to be accepted, many of us have qualities that others might find to be peculiar. This is what makes life all the more interesting and yet it can be the source of much animosity and unrest. Just because something has not been your experience does not make it any less true, at least to the person who has experienced it. On the other hand, we cannot be consumed with trying to prove ourselves to everyone else. While there are certain irrefutable laws that apply, what I believe often becomes true for me and what you believe often becomes true for you. When something resonates, I know it by the sensations that arise within my body and from my deeper awareness.

By attuning to our inner wisdom, I believe that we can transcend judgments and beliefs that seek to control, divide, belittle, justify hatred and any form of prejudice. We practice discernment when we observe and form thoughtful conclusions from a place of compassion and humility, honoring all aspects of ourselves, the situation at hand, as well as any others who might be involved. If something does not resonate or feel in alignment with the best in me, then I must adhere to that guidance. Still, I pay attention even after a decision has been made. I observe when anything new arises.

Being receptive to life

There are times when life provides an opportunity to see from an entirely different perspective. As someone who became deaf and blind after an illness when she was just a toddler, Helen Keller *(June 27, 1880 ~ June 1, 1968)* said it best. "When one door of happiness closes, another opens; but often we look so long at the closed door that we do not see the one which has opened for us." Doors are always closing and opening. It is up to each of us to choose whether to walk through or not.

> Dream Journal: February 1, 2010...*I am in an unfamiliar place and I find myself waiting. It is not clear who or what I am waiting for. I then hear a gentle tapping at the door. I approach the door but stand before it in silence.*
>
> *My pulse quickens as I wait. I make no attempt to answer the knock until a voice whispers, "It is me." This is when I open the door.*

This dream was symbolic of all that was happening during that period of my life. I had been faced with a life-altering decision—something I had emphatically said "no" to at an earlier time. A childhood friend had offered to be a gestational surrogate for my husband and me after multiple miscarriages and two pre-term birth losses, but I would not consider it at first. *That is not the way nature intended it,* was my initial thought. *A child should be created out of love,* I had said in response to her offer.

In time, my perspective began to shift and I recognized that this was truly an act of love. A trusted friend was willing to help me in bringing another desired child into the world. *Why would I not accept this gift?* I had to replace a long-held dream of a *natural* childbirth experience I once imagined. This would also be the ultimate lesson in letting go. So much would be beyond my control. The series of legal and medical steps seemed enormous. Still, after months of introspection, research, guidance, and prayer, it then felt right to walk through this new door that had opened up to us. Saying yes to this process was creating an opportunity for new life. It was an opening to another experience that the hand of grace seemed to be extending in our direction.

But after two unsuccessful outcomes, we again had to re-adjust to a different reality. "The odds are in your favor," the doctor had originally said. I knew there were no guarantees, but I truly had not considered this daunting possibility. *Why then were we led down this road of uncertainty?*

It was on April 10, 2013 when we said the words aloud—neither of us wanted to proceed with the final embryo transfer. We had already been through so much and the risk of another disappointment seemed too much to bear. Five months passed, and we still had not alerted the facility of our decision. As it turned out, we didn't have to. They called us instead. Actually, the call came to my cell phone. I was in the middle of a conversation with neighbors, my cousin and another friend, awaiting the school bus. I was not prepared for this phone call, but I am grateful for the persons who were with me. I did not have to hide my tears.

Most days I am confident that we made the best decision we could at that time. My grandmother had visited me in a dream (March 2, 2013). In this dream, she showed me a photograph of a white dove. I watched as the dove became animated within the picture. The dove flew a short distance, and then it stopped. She showed me a second photo of a white dove taking flight and then abruptly coming to a stop. She was about to show me a third photo when someone else entered the room. Instead of showing me the third picture, she looked at me and shook her head, indicating no.

Yet, there are more vulnerable times when a wave of sadness wells up and the tears begin to fall, especially when I recall a conversation with my daughter.

"I feel like I've lost someone," she shared one evening. The school year had just begun, fourth grade, a new school, in a new town—it made sense that she might be missing some of her friends and former classmates.

"No mom, it feels like it's someone from my family, but I don't know who it is," she insisted.

A comforting hug was all that I could offer.

But then a few days later, during the early morning hours, it was as though her words, *"No, mom it feels like someone from my family…"* suddenly collided with the words spoken by the person from the fertility center, *"the embryo will be discarded."* As I re-read my journal pages from that morning, even years later, it is still painful to relive this moment. I am choosing to share only fragments, enough to illustrate the array of emotions experienced when we begin to question our most difficult decisions. Feel free to skip this next entry.

Acknowledging the experience: September 24, 2013…*and to know that she might be sensing this loss…there is a sinking feeling in my heart…Did we do the right thing? …Discarded…as in thrown away… Why was this choice ours to make? Were there other options? I should* *have let it go to voicemail…*

Processing the emotions: *September 25, 2013…I didn't feel you growing inside me, but I felt you in my soul. This time, I did not hold you, but I held you in my heart. There is a deep sense of loss because I hoped you would be. For a brief moment you were. It is hard to think a part of me has died. I would rather believe that a part of me lived…*

When I now sort through my emotions, I do so not to assign blame. Instead, the intention is to carve a path to my deeply held values and certitudes. Having made the decision at a previous time in a more peaceful state, not clouded by emotion is what allowed my husband and me to move forward. Still, it is interesting how many other scenarios easily materialize long after the fact. It might have been reasonable to ask to discuss with the doctor at a later time when my husband could also be present. Maybe I should have let the call go to voicemail. And maybe, everything is as it could only have been.

Living forward

September 25, 2013…Tonight I light this candle. I open my heart and set this encapsulated energy free. You are more than a thought, more than an unrealized dream. You are more than a cluster of cells. You are a spark of creation, a tender piece of my heart. As you return to Spirit, I will rest in the peaceful knowing that energy can never be destroyed. I didn't hold you in my arms, but I will continue to hold you in my heart…

As I embraced the reality of *what is* rather than what might have been, there was a sense of peace. It was then that I recognized that I must choose to live this day forward, allowing past decisions to be what they were, serving as wisdom to guide future decision-making. I can only make decisions based on who I am in the moment, not based on what others might think or how I expect to feel at a later time. *Allow the heaviness of the past to fall away* I hear from within. This reminds me of a quote offered by Pierre Teilhard de Chardin *(May 1, 1881 ~ April 10, 1955)* in *Hymn of the Universe.* He wrote, "A heavy cloak slipped from his shoulders and fell to the ground behind him; the dead weight of all that is false, narrow, tyrannical, all that is artificially contrived…" My body tingles as I re-read these words.

Choosing love

My experiences through pregnancy loss and preterm births have broadened and shaped my views in ways I never would have imagined. When I was told at twenty-one weeks gestation that the safest option for me would be to have labor induced, I chose otherwise. This was just after hearing my baby's heartbeat and being told that it was strong and that his movement was good. I still remember the compassionate nurse who said, "Miracles happen." If there was any possibility of his survival, I wanted to give him that chance. I am grateful for having that choice. Without intervention, preterm labor did progress and this pregnancy ended. I then experienced life-threatening complications, requiring several blood transfusions without informed consent. It was a life or death and my doctors chose to keep me alive. I am grateful that they made that choice.

In recent years, there has been much conflict surrounding the concepts of pro-life and pro-choice. *How does one choose a side?* I cannot be strictly "pro-life" without recognizing that life is about making choices and I am grateful for every freedom that I enjoy. I cannot be strictly "pro-choice" without realizing that every life has purpose and meaning. Therefore, I choose love and respect. I choose to make the best possible decisions I can for myself, for my daughter, for our family. I choose to guide her in practicing *good* judgment and how to be discerning as she navigates this wondrous world. And, I choose to allow others the freedom to do what feels right for them and enables them to live their lives fully without malice to another.

Whenever we judge someone, something or an experience, we narrow the view not only of that person or thing or experience, but we also narrow the view of who we are. As Mother Teresa *(August 26, 1910 ~ September 5, 1997)* would say, "If you judge people, you have no time to love them." Likewise, when you judge yourself or judge what you experience, you spend less time loving yourself and you are less open to the experience. A heart filled with love and compassion remains open to life, open to change and open to wonder. To be inhabited by love opens us up to limitless potential and infinite possibility. And when we are truly open, we are better able to see people as they are, not as we wish them to be. We see the true expression of ourselves, our shared story and the greater truth in all that we experience. It is then that we all can be free.

Love

~ PRACTICE ~

Creating a Sacred Space

An altar can be a sacred space that represents and honors all that you are. It is a place that invites you to elevate your thoughts and shift your energy when needed. Select items that signify love, hope, inspiration, peace and calm. Your altar may hold a source of light like a candle or a crystal. It might display a rock or a gemstone or a small container of water from your favorite beach, lake or stream. It might hold a single flower, a memento that belonged to a grandparent or a photo of an ancestor. You might display a prayer, a handwritten letter, a painting or postcard.

Stand before your altar with your cares and worries, your graces and gratitudes. Stand before your altar and breathe in its inspiration. In the words of the Dalai Lama, "As you breathe in, cherish yourself. As you breathe out, cherish all beings." Offer your hopes and dreams for yourself, a loved one, the world we live in. Breathe in love, breathe out love.

The voice within says,

I am open to life and to new experiences that guide me to wholeness. I choose to participate in my own healing, the healing of others and the healing of this world. I choose Life. I choose freedom. I choose love.

Insight: Embracing Life, Discovering Beauty, Grace and True Purpose

Chapter 3

Vitality

As I begin the writing of this chapter, I close my eyes with a notebook and pen in hand, awaiting whatever arises. An image from a recent dream begins to surface. At first, I do not see its relevance to the principle of vitality—*exuberant physical strength and mental vigor; the capacity for the continuation of a meaningful and purposeful existence* as defined by Dictionary.com.

> Dream Journal: January 23, 2020...*I am standing alone in my backyard. Through the dark of this night, I notice a bat. Instead of hanging from the tree branch, the bat stands upright, facing the lake. To the right of the bat is a lantern with a brilliant glow. I notice that the lantern and the bat are of similar height and width. The bat's right wing extends as if to hold the lantern. I also observe the lake. There is stillness, no moonlight, just*

the glow from the lantern.

It is not often that my dreams defy natural laws—an upright bat when bats are not capable of standing and a lantern steady atop a tree branch. As I described the elements of this dream to one friend, *the darkness holds the light* seemed to be an obvious message. I found myself curious about the significance of looking towards the East. This is when another friend introduced me to a book, *Medicine Cards: The Discovery of Power through the Ways of Animals*, teachings based on the collective wisdom of Aztec, Cherokee, Cheyenne, Choctaw, Iroquois, Lakota, Mayan, Seneca and Yaqui traditions.

Indigenous medicine encompasses just about anything that brings us into harmony with the natural world, honoring everything as a teacher, allowing us to see our vast connection to all of life, all that is known to us, and all that remains a mystery. Not only was I intrigued by the symbolism of the bat totem expressed in this book, but I also came across explanations for the cardinal directions (East, West, North, and South) as they relate to the position of the animal totems, which also proved useful for my interpretation of this dream. There are seven directions described in this text written by Jamie Sams (Cherokee and Seneca descent) and David Carson (Choctaw descent). The following is the ancient guidance provided for the direction of East.

> **East:** The animal in the East guides you to your greatest spiritual challenges and guards your path to illumination.

This called to mind my first encounter with the Great Blue Heron while contemplating Dr. Wayne Dyer's teachings. This graceful bird had made its presence known to the West of where I was seated. This is what *Medicine Cards* has to say:

> **West:** The animal in the West leads you
> to your personal truth and inner answers.
> It also shows you the path to your goals.

Navigating uncertainty

Not only are bats adaptable and guided by their perception of things that others might not see, but the bat also symbolizes a boundless cycle of facing our shadows, releasing non-essential patterns and beginning anew. At the time of this writing, the world appears to be in a significant gestation period due to a pandemic. What at first seemed to be a welcomed opportunity to pause and rest for a moment has been extended. We have been asked to remain inside and await a new beginning. For many, but not all of us, our homes, much like a womb, provide a haven. For all of us, there is much uncertainty as we seek to determine what is essential and non-essential for ourselves, our families and our larger community.

Where there is uncertainty, there can be much anxiety and overwhelm, lethargy and trepidation. What will life look like on the other side of this? No one really knows. We still have to live through it. It helps to remember that with uncertainty comes a myriad of possibilities that do not have to be all bad. Where there is uncertainty, there is also opportunity for compassion and courage, patience and humility, resilience and creativity.

Transcending Betrayal

This extended pause might seem like a betrayal. Many of us who take good care of our bodies are disoriented by the fear that we or someone we love could succumb to illness at any moment. Many who have sacrificed a great deal for well-earned positions must now procure new means of providing for their families. Those who provide a much-needed service must close their doors for an indeterminate period. Those of us deemed essential are confronted with other challenges as we navigate this time of crisis.

Anxiety...

I used to view anxiety as a betrayer whenever it crept up and surged throughout my body. Trying not to be anxious would only make it worse. Now, I pay attention when an anxious thought first arrives. I pause and I listen. It is usually tied to some future event or something beyond my immediate control as in these current times. I listen to hear what this sense of anxiety has to say as I breathe deeply, resting one hand on my forehead and the other at the back. I then reach for my journal or contact a friend. *Do not live it before it happens,* a wise friend once advised. *Help me to accept the things I cannot change,* the Serenity Prayer offers. *How about we watch a romantic comedy together,* I might now say to this anxiousness within my body. Before too long, one of us falls asleep.

I have come to accept that I am one of those persons who must be diligent about self-care. There are times when I wish I could stay up late or watch a popular thriller that gets my heart racing, but that is not my reality. Although I wish to stay informed, I must also limit my exposure to certain television images and broadcasts. I once shared a post where someone wrote, "sensitivity is my superpower." But my truth is, having extreme sensitivity to the happenings of the world does not always feel like a gift. I am most grateful for all the techniques and practices I have gathered and shared over the years. And as a friend of a friend says, "I only watch the news to know where to send the angels."

Learning to breathe again

Where there is breath, there is reason for living. Where there is life, there is more to the evolving story of hope, healing and our becoming. Amid whatever is happening, our breath is one thing we can connect to and modulate. When I breathe deeply, I find my center and begin to live more connected to this moment, right here, right now, where I am safe. When I consciously slow my breath, my trust in the goodness of life is restored. I am better able to face a future no one can fully predict. I become aware that I exist as a part of a much greater whole—that my breath is the life force of all who existed before me; all who loved me into being. I breathe in their love and remember their resilience. Breath is vital. Gratitude is vital. Trust is vital. The strength of my faith is vital to me. As Rabbi Steve Leder offers, "Faith does not cure disease, but it heals despair."

Remembering your resilience

When it comes to any form of betrayal we still have a choice; to become a victim of unfortunate circumstance or to harness our vitality and extract the resilience that we were born out of. Our ancestors, women and men, left shores of comfort and familiarity to embrace a more magnificent dream for their lives. There were the ones who determined which berries were safe and which ones would put us to sleep. They were the ones to escape bondage in order to experience greater freedoms that their predecessors only dreamed of. They were the ones to plot a new course and set sail without certainty of when or where they would come ashore. They likely got lost a few times, but somehow managed to find their way. And a great many of them accepted life's detours as opportunities to build something entirely different and just as wonderful.

How we respond to stress and traumatic circumstances is not just a matter of our survival. These moments set the stage for novel innovations and extraordinary ways of being. Sir Arthur Charles Clarke (*December 16, 1917 ~ March 19, 2008*), a science fiction writer once proclaimed, "The only way to discover the limits of the possible is to go beyond them into the impossible." Challenging times, more than anything else, propels us into the impossible. It might have seemed unlikely to venture unto a new career path and yet this is the reality for many people at this present moment.

Live this day!

We become empowered when we make the decision to live this day. We do not know how tomorrow will be, but how we choose to live today matters. We can still choose hope over despair, faith over fear, begin anew rather than relive the pain of betrayal. We either accept people as they are, or we love them at a distance. "People know themselves better than you do," explains Dr. Maya Angelou (*April 4, 1928 ~ May 28, 2014*). "That's why it's important to stop expecting them to be something other than who they are." As difficult as it might be to part ways when differences cause unrelenting pain, to keep these persons in close proximity could be the ultimate betrayal to oneself. Unfortunately, some marriages end. This temporary union served as an opportunity for two people to grow together and they journeyed as far as they were physically meant to. To move forward without resentment and bitterness maintains the love once shared and paves the way for healing. "This day I married my friend," and this day we chose to be better friends.

We must also recognize when our past actions have been the source of another's hurt and disappointment. Even though the hurt was unintentional, the pain must be acknowledged and reconciled whenever possible. Life offers us an array of experiences to see ourselves more clearly. "When you know better, you do better," Dr. Angelou also encourages. We can all resolve to do better from this day forward.

Likewise, when life appears to stray from our well-crafted plans, we have to find our way through the meandering darkness. I wrote to a friend on January 18, 2010:

> *I will forever be a mother of nine souls.*
> *Four of their hearts, I have heard beating.*
> *I have held three of them and looked upon their faces. And one of them, God has placed within my care, for now.*

Though I continue to believe that everything ultimately weaves together for good, while in the throes of suffering, it can be difficult to maintain that everything serves a purpose. Time alone does not heal, yet adequate time is a necessary component. Healing does not always occur instantaneously. Perspective, self-compassion and loving support are also required in order to expand beyond the hurt and emerge with greater strength.

Acknowledging the experience: September 15, 2006...*How could I...a health conscious, deeply spiritual and guided by faith, happy-to-be-pregnant, thirty-two-year-old mother of one...not be able to carry this baby to term...How could a body that I have taken such good care of, fail me? This doesn't make sense.*

Ten months later...

Processing the emotions: July 18, 2007...*As I sit here, there is a gentle breeze. Not only does the sunlight seem brighter, but it also feels just a little bit warmer, or maybe I now feel more deeply. Voices echo louder and at times silence seems deafening or it might be that I now listen more closely. The world has changed for me, but not for everyone else. It seems a bit unfair, or maybe this is just how it's meant to be. The world seems different, but maybe it has stayed the same and I am the one who is forever changed.*

Healing is a process. It takes as long as it takes. We must live this day and the next day and the ones after that. Eventually, we string together enough days to look back and see that somehow it all made sense.

Aliveness!

Civil rights leader Howard Washington Thurman *(November 18, 1899 ~ April 10, 1981)* would say that the world yearns for more of us "who have come alive." Vitality is about aliveness, not just survival. While our bodies, by design, are self-healing and regenerative, this process is not the same for every person. Healing can come in ways we would never expect. For me, unexplained pregnancy challenges were the impetus for further immersion into integrative health, various mind-body modalities, personal growth exploration and a deepening spiritual practice, all of which transformed not only my health and well-being, but have also benefitted my family, friends and many of my patients. Recurring loss has given rise to even more life within me. From this vantage point, I can now say that it could not have happened any other way.

I have also come to see that we do not get our lives all neat and tidy and expect that it stays that way, indefinitely. Life is ever-evolving with opportunities to further heal and grow. The question I now ask is *"how can I be most at peace as I live through these moments?* My prayer is *thank you for all that I am and yet to become.* Shrouded in the mystery of every experience, there is always something meaningful that we can give rise to.

Embracing the mystery

"We don't know what happened, but you're still here because you were healthy." These were the words spoken with humility by one my attending intensive care physicians. I had experienced a complication known as disseminated intravascular coagulation (DIC) which affects the blood's ability to clot, resulting in the loss of more than fifty percent of my blood volume. This doctor affirmed that my body's ability to survive a life-threatening emergency was due to the fact that I had been in good health. Hearing his words, *"you're still here…"* allowed me to release the previously held belief that my body had failed me.

When our bodies do not function as they were designed to, it is difficult not to take it personally. We can do all the *right* things and still not be able to carry a pregnancy to term. We can avoid all the *wrong* things and still experience health challenges. There is much that is beyond our immediate control and yet we can listen to the messages of our body and care for it as best we can. Miracles still happen. In her book, *Dying to Be Me: My Journey from Cancer to near Death to True Healing*, Anita Moorjani shares how she ate "very healthfully" prior to her diagnosis of cancer, but that she did so out of fear. This was a great reminder for me to check in and assess my motivations for my *healthy* habits. I also see the truth in what Anita Moorjani says, "Everyone has a purpose, regardless of their physical condition."

"Science cannot solve the ultimate mystery of nature," wrote German physicist Max Planck (*April 23, 1858 ~ October 4, 1947*). We observe. We explore. We do our best to uncover the mystery and yet, "…we ourselves are a part of the mystery…" While we may not understand all the underpinnings of this world, one thing is for certain; we are each a vital part of this unfolding mystery.

Nourish your heart with laughter

It makes a difference how well we care for ourselves, finding ways to nourish our heart as well as our physical body and mind. When we can look beyond a surmounting challenge and notice a heart-shaped puddle, a budding daffodil or the wondrous eyes of a child, we bring lightness to our hearts. When we can find humor and laugh at the absurdity of a situation, we bring much needed calm to our nervous system. We feel more grounded. When we laugh, we strengthen our resolve to keep moving lifeward.

Love

Even after a particularly difficult day, I wanted to keep to my daughter's bedtime ritual of reading with her. She suggested that we read, "Neerg Sgee Dna Mah." She knew I would not willingly read *Green Eggs and Ham* yet again that week. Her cleverness in attempting to say the words of the title backwards caused me to laugh. She then thought it would be fun to read the entire book this way. I agreed to reading the sentences in reverse order so "I do not like them" became "them like not do I." Before long, we were laughing hysterically at our silliness. This moment did not change the events of the day, but it allowed for a restful night's sleep.

~ PRACTICE ~

Embodying the Vitality of Water

A bath is one of the best ways to embody the vitalizing properties of this water. Using dried rose petals, essential rose oil or a combination of both, create a healing bath with the addition of Himalayan salt or Epsom salt. You might choose to do a foot bath or decide to immerse yourself fully.

Be softened, allowing yourself to become as fluid and as flexible, dissolving and releasing all that is beyond your control. Be soothed as you feel yourself being wrapped in the arms of grace. "I believe that water is the closest thing to a god we have here on Earth," wrote Alex Moores in his novel *Living in Water*. We are in awe of its power and majestic beauty. We are drawn to it as if it's a magical, healing force."

The voice within says,

Vitality flows from the depths of my innermost being as I give and receive love. I express my deepest gratitude to the Source of all creation and all of the ancestors, human and otherwise, who guide my dreams and experiences.

Chapter 4

Essence

"You look better than you did yesterday. Looks like you're gonna be okay." He is an older gentleman, mopping the floors of my hospital room in intensive care. I look up with an attempted smile before my eyes fall back to my sheets. "You're gonna be okay," he says again in a gentle, yet commanding tone. This time he stops mopping and stands at the foot of the bed as my eyes lift again to meet with his. Eventually, I nod in agreement. For some unknown reason, I believe him. A stranger with no reason to care for my well-being is the one person able to convince me that I would survive this harrowing experience. He goes back to mopping and more than ten years later, I easily recall this brief exchange.

While I cannot be certain I would recognize this man if ever our paths were to converge again, I remember his essence, marked by compassion and assuredness. I imagine he must have been a grandfather. Grandfathers have that way of telling you how it's going to be without being overbearing. I wonder if he knew how essential he was to this intensive care unit, not only for his physical duties, but also for his presence. He was essential to my healing. I imagine he was a healing presence to many others.

What is essential to who you are?

> *"If we don't know who we are, then we are whoever somebody says we are"*
>
> ~Amos N. Wilson, African American Psychologist,
>
> *(February 23, 1941~January 14, 1995)*

Our essence is that aspect of our inner being that is always present within us and yet it is what we leave behind with those we encounter. It is that identifiable *something* that without it, we could not be exactly as we are. *What makes you, you?* It is what is left at your core when all the layers of conditioning have been peeled away. Essence is also what allows the Earth, the oceans and the stars to exist within us. According to American astronomer, Carl Sagan (*November 9, 1934 ~ December 20, 1996*), "The nitrogen in our DNA, the calcium in our teeth, the iron in our blood...we are made of star stuff. We are a way for the cosmos to know itself." And if the essence of earth, the oceans and stars exist within us—so does the essence of those who once were. Here upon this earth and within us, a part of them will forever remain.

Krista...

Early one morning (May 25, 2012), I was still in bed and could faintly hear my daughter calling, "Mom." I was not awake enough to answer, but I heard her call for me a second time. It was not a cry or an alarming call. She was eight and self-sufficient. I was drifting back to sleep when an image of Krista's face appeared in my mind which startled me awake. I immediately jumped out of bed and went into the adjacent bathroom. My daughter was in there, standing.

We were talking and all of a sudden she says, "Why can't I see anything," and begins to lose consciousness. I caught her in time and lowered her to the floor, calling her name, no idea of what was happening, trying my best not to panic. She awoke within a minute or two. The paramedics were already on the way. They checked her vitals and a follow-up visit to her pediatrician confirmed that she was well. I do not want to imagine what could have happened had I not gotten out of bed when I did. Thankfully, I do not have to. Vasovagal syncope was the only diagnosis. *Thank you, Krista.*

How is it that Krista's face appeared to me that morning? There was no apparent reason for her to come to mind at that particular moment. My book signing had been held in March, about two months prior to this day. I had met with the director of the *Samaritans* on April 18, 2012 and had decided it was not a good fit. There was no rational explanation for my vision of her that morning, yet the timing was important to my daughter's well-being.

Understanding your visions

What I refer to as visions occur most often when I am between wakefulness and sleep. To describe it as accurately as possible, it is a state of being somewhat conscious, yet not focused on a particular thought. Scenes begin to play out in my mind, without my direction. And then one or more details hold my attention, causing me to become more fully awake.

In April of 2011, I spent a weekend in Quebec at a retreat center known as Terre Nouvelle. On the first night, I was drifting into sleep when I envisioned a conversation with one of the other workshop attendees who appeared to be of Indian descent. Thoughts of my biological father entered my mind. I never knew him although he was not a complete stranger to my mom's family. I was told he was not a *pleasant* man. In March 2009, when I inquired about him after a dream I had, I learned that he had died sometime in 1997.

The following morning at breakfast, the gentleman who had been in my vision approached me and we had a conversation. When I mentioned I was originally from the Caribbean, he replied, "I have friends from the island of Trinidad." The man who fathered me was Trinidadian. This synchronicity prompted me to write a letter that evening.

Acknowledging the experience: Journal entry: April 30, 2011…A Letter to My…*What of you is in me? I exist in part because of you. So, by definition, you are my father. I never knew you although you knew of me. I do not love you, but I don't despise you either. It makes me sad to know that I was not created out of love. How is it that I can love so deeply in spite of this? I was not loved by you, but I was loved. I was not created out of your love, but I was created out of God's love. My hope is that the best of you is in me. That is all. Goodnight.*

Transcending Abandonment

Many of us look to our parents and sometimes our significant others to determine who we are and how we are meant to exist in this life. The landscape of abandonment, physical or emotional, whether it occurs in childhood or adulthood, does not diminish our truest essence nor does it dictate our continuing story. And yet, if we strongly feel the void of their absence, we might begin to question our worth. *Who am I because of the man who fathered me? Is there any part of him that loved me? Why was he not present in my life?*

I had often wondered how my life would have been different had my biology been different. I was twelve when I first learned that my dad who raised me was not my biological father. At first, I felt like an outsider—like I was the one who did not belong. Now, I recognize that it is not only how we come into existence or what happens throughout our lives, but also the choices we make in spite of our beginnings—how we adapt and grow and become more iridescent versions of ourselves. Our biology signals our physical expression, but who be become is the sum of our experiences and our choices.

Everything is a teacher

Just like the formation of a pearl in the belly of an oyster, it seems that we are all born and adopted into circumstances necessary to excavate our essence and to realize our fullest potential. Pain happens to be the most thorough excavator, breaking us open and exposing our depths in a way nothing else can. How that pain gets transmuted—well that is up to each of us.

The abandoned can still make a choice not to abandon themselves or another person. The abused can decide not to self-harm or be abusive toward others. The rejected can choose self-respect and see the inherent worth and dignity in every other person. Dr. Wayne Dyer sums it up well, "Look upon every experience you've ever had, and everyone who's ever played any role in your life, as having been sent to you for your benefit."

We are all branches of the same tree

Is it that simple—to just decide not to do what has been done to us; to choose a path other than the one that was laid out for us to walk upon? I suppose it can be that way for some. For most of us, it comes with practice. We can adopt a practice of awareness, action and accompaniment.

AWARENESS: *What I do to you, I have also done to me.* We are all branches of the same tree, derived from a constant source of all that is good. This goodness is often obscured when circumstances give rise to negative emotions such as inadequacy, bitterness and disconnection. The intense emotions fuel further malevolence. Those who inflict harm are often acting out of a self-centered approach to getting their needs met or they might gain some satisfaction in drawing others into their misery. Those who feel powerless might seek out ways to exert force over someone else. Those consumed by bitterness are quicker to spew insults. This helps us see the true in the words, *it is not about you*. It is that person's own sufferings that is at the root of their caustic comments and behavior. Constantly being aware of our truest essence reminds us to adopt our own personal oath of "do no harm," which allows us to respond with benevolence.

ACTION: *I cannot change the actions of another, but I am accountable for my own.* Whether a cycle gets broken or repeated is dependent on our present actions. What we do in this moment can have far reaching consequences beyond the emotional trauma that impacted us. We are powerfully creative beings and as branches of the same tree, how we continue to grow and evolve will be dependent on whether our actions serve our highest expression. Will you remain in bondage, chained to the past or will you set out onto a more favorable road?

ACCOMPANIMENT: *I do not have to do this life alone.* We all need supportive, reliable, objective persons to accompany us on the journey from our past into a more promising future. The past cannot be anything other than what it is. The future, however, is yet to be created. Not only was Rome not built in a day. It also most certainly was not created alone.

Processing the emotions: Journal entry: May 1, 2011…*Terre Nouvelle. It is here that I have been able to see that although I was not created out of romantic love, I was created out of God's love. There is a sense of belonging—of coming home. I feel a connection, not only to this group, but to others who wish to become whole and facilitate the healing of this beautiful earth. Drinking from the wellspring this weekend deepened my connection and love for the earth and for all humanity. I am like an obedient child, but no longer out of fear. This obedience is due to my trust in the goodness of life and in our compassion as human beings. We were all given gifts unique to our journey—Gifts that were not intended to be kept hidden away. These treasures were meant to be unearthed and intended for us to share.*

How might I serve?

*I, the fiery life of divine essence…I
awaken everything to life.*

~Hildegard of Bingen *(c. 1098* ~

September 17, 1179)

Nothing lived is ever without purpose. Those who have experienced poverty are better able to understand those who struggle to meet their basic needs for love, food and shelter. Those who have felt trapped are charged with helping others to set themselves free. Those who have endured much pain are able to recognize the pain in others; so, that is where they can best serve.

Divine guidance though human voices

Moments after leading our group in a Qigong meditation, I was approached by one of the founders of Terre Nouvelle. "You are going to bring people together," she affirms as we embrace. She is a petite woman, but only in stature. Her inner resolve is palpable. This was after another participant offered me these words, "My word for you would be fertility." He obviously had no idea of my pregnancy journey. And yet I was touched by this sentiment.

Take a moment to reflect on someone who has helped you to recognize the core of your essence. *What did they see in you that you were hesitant to see in yourself?* "At times our own light goes out and is rekindled by a spark from another person," German theologian Albert Schweitzer *(January 14, 1875 ~ September 4, 1965)* would say. "Each of us has cause to think with deep gratitude of those who have lighted the flame within us." *Thank you for sharing this, Reverend Daniel.*

Love

~ PRACTICE ~

Embodying the Essence of a Tree

Trees are some of our nearest ancestors. Listen to what they have to say. Sit or stand nearby or beneath one. Focus your awareness on the fact that this tree is anchored to the ground and supported by roots that absorb life-sustaining water, minerals and other nutrients. This tree has a solid core. It has branches that extend outwards and upwards.

ROOTS: What defines your root system? In other words, what do you need to grow and evolve into the best version of yourself? What keeps you grounded? What nourishes and sustains you? A Spiritual Source? Silence? Mountains? Proximity to water? Sand and Sea? Love of learning? Beauty found in the natural world? Strong family ties? Knowledge of self? Movement? Dance?

CORE: What is at your core? What quality most defines your essence, without it, you could not be all that you are. Calmness? Curiosity? Creativity? Determination? Docility to divine guidance? Generosity? Gentleness? Humor? Kindness? Love of Adventure? Love of Children? Love of Community? Reverence for all of life?

BRANCHES: Consider your branches that extend upwards and outwards. How might you serve? What do you wish to give? What do you wish to receive? Beauty? Creativity? Compassion? Freedom? Generosity? Gentleness? Healing? Hope? Humor? Honesty? Inspiration? Justice? Kindness? Peace? Presence? Protection? Prosperity? Wisdom?

The voice within says,

I am divinity realized, created for evolving purpose. I am the student and the teacher, docile to divine guidance, deeply respectful of all life. I extend my branches to inspire hope, healing and becoming free. I am healed as I heal. My truest essence is love.

Chapter 5

Harmony

It is interesting to be writing about harmony at a time when the present world (May 17, 2020) appears to be in a state of disharmony. Each day, conflicting voices echo thoughts of how we should exist moment to moment. The divisiveness is palpable on many platforms. *How do I remain centered when fear and confusion abound? How do I continue to respond with compassion and not become reactive?* I recognize that frustration and resentment only impede forward movement and clarity.

Observe the beauty inherent in nature

This period has allowed me to spend more hours each day with the natural world. For the first time, I notice a pattern of tiny white flowers with yellow centers in a grassy area. Are they considered to be weeds just because they add a fleeting variation to the usual landscape? Nature seems to make room for all its imperfections scattered about the tree branches and patches of grass. Each tree stands firm in its uniqueness. Each stone seems to have found its rightful place. I watch as an eagle circles high above reminding me to keep my thoughts elevated. These words arise:

> *Like a prism, life offers parallel planes intended to deepen one's understanding of all that is. Remain curious. Allow the waters of sadness and the fires of anger to carve new channels and paths to other meaningful experiences. Be faithful. There is good in all things.*

I sit on the ground and allow this message to occupy me. I recall a phrase from Shakespeare's, *As You Like It*. "And this, our life, exempt from public haunt, finds tongues in trees, books in the running brooks, sermons in stones, and good in everything." ~William Shakespeare (*c.1564 ~April 23, 1616*). I imagine how Shakespeare spent hours among the trees, listening, observing, contemplating, being and finding the good in everything.

Listen to the space between...

To be in harmony requires that we seek ways to exist not only with nature, but also with one another. We must remember that we share this generous Earth with other life forms. Should we not extend that generosity whenever we can? To exist harmoniously, we must find what unites us and overcome what divides. How? Where do we begin sifting and sorting through the copious information that is provided daily? *Listen to the space*, the wisdom from within and beyond writes.

Like the space between musical notes, listen to the space between the words. Listen for what is left unspoken as well as to what is spoken. What is the intention of the words as they fall upon your ears? Feel the energy of these words. Where do they land in your body? Do they trigger your need for safety and security? Do they fall into your solar plexus and leave you feeling empowered or disempowered? Do they incite fear and anxiety or inspire hope and trust? Do they captivate? Intrigue or prompt eye rolling? Soothe or frighten? Confuse or clarify? Listen to the space.

Observe how you experience this space. If there is discomfort, how can you respond to the discomfort with dignity, honoring all that you are? If there is a sense of hopefulness, how can you cultivate more of that hope in yourself and in others? If this prompts eye rolling, where in you do you feel resistance? Is the resistance coming from deep within or from a place of skepticism?

I was sent a video one evening and asked to share my thoughts about its content. I immediately watched the video but felt too tired to respond. The next morning, I awoke with the phrase "double-doubles" as though it was a remnant of a dream. It turns out that a *double-double* is a performance-based term used in basketball to describe when a player scores double digits in two of five categories. Was my dream literally speaking to the overall validity of the video, saying that while it scored in two categories, they were still three other areas where it missed the mark? Was the exhaustion I felt after listening a greater clue about the vibration of what was being conveyed? Or was I simply just tired?

My response to the video via text, "*…my sense is that we are not to live in fear but practice good judgment and honor our innermost wisdom. There is so much overwhelming information and I believe that the truth or versions of the truth lie somewhere in the midst of it all.*

We each have to determine from a place of peace what feels true for ourselves and those we care about."

Just two days later, May 10, 2020, I awoke with the words, *"I do love a good intrigue."* We are often fascinated by stories of deception as well as stories that allude to impropriety and leave us with more questions than answers. Being aware of this helps me to remain curious yet discerning about what I hear and read. While it is often helpful to reach out for the opinions of others we trust, it is also imperative to connect to our own inner sense.

Diversity allows for greater harmony

Harmony is about balancing multiple components. Diverse voices and opinions add to the conversation and allow us to maintain a balanced view of our world. When we lean too far to any one side, we exclude the ideas and views of others that could lend perspective to our collective challenges. Is it possible for multiple versions of the truth to exist simultaneously? Can multiple experts have varying opinions? Is science infallible? Does censorship really protect? Would it not be more prudent to present all of the information, share best practices and allow every able-minded individual to choose? What if another person's choices impact you or your family? Then, what practices can you put into place that assures greater protection for yourself and your loved ones?

When something resonates, it serves to confirm and clarify what is true for me in a given moment. What is true for me today may not necessarily be true tomorrow, but I have to live this day as best I can with the knowledge that is currently available. Growth and wisdom allow for changes in beliefs and modifications of behavior. Likewise, dissonance cautions me to sort through the opinions of others that inform and guide my decision-making. While I cannot control the choices and behavior of others, I can still make choices, deciding to keep my distance, imposing limits on the amount of time, if at all, spent with certain persons. As in music, sometimes there is a greater space between the notes, allowing the melody to rest and adding to the overall harmony of the song.

Still, it is my belief that every voice holds an important element that is needed for our collective well-being. We cannot disregard an opinion simply because it does not conform to our current understanding. As Andre Rochais would say, "We are asleep on a gold mine, on a wellspring of energy, on a volcano of creativity. Everything is there, in the hidden corners of humanity, in the interior recesses of men and women throughout the planet." Wisdom can be found in every voice on this planet, even the ones we rarely agree with.

Transcending Envy

According to the enneagram, a system of identifying personality types based on motivations and patterns of behavior, I resonate most with type Four. Fours are often described as the Romantic Individualist with the need to understand and be understood. According to *My Best Self: Using the Enneagram to Free the Soul* by Kathleen Hurley and Theodore Dobson, Fours seek to camouflage their original wound of abandonment and their shortcoming is envy, always comparing ourselves to everyone else. For the longest while, I thought I was a type Two, the helpers. However, I now understand that when Fours are on a path of stress and disintegration, they compensate by becoming "over-involved" in helping everyone else.

> Dream journal: May 18, 2020…*We are in a familiar home, but there are noticeable differences such as the placement of furniture and appliances. We politely greet each other but exchange few words. I notice her blouse. It has a white background with a beautiful print of black vines, flowers and leaves. When she turns away from me, I notice a single red leaf in the lower right corner.*

Now days later (May 22, 2020), flipping through pages of a coloring journal with designs surrounding mostly lined pages, I opened to a page resembling the pattern of the blouse that appeared in my dream. I purchased this journal years ago. The cover reads, "Beauty Lives in Nature." Oddly enough, the background of the page I opened to is black, while the vines, flowers and leaves are white. This is in complete contrast to how the pattern appeared in my dream—a similar pattern, but what was black is white and what was white is black.

What exists in you also exists in me

Acknowledging the experience: May 22, 2020…*It occurs to me that while I admired her blouse, I did not compliment her. What comes to mind is a moment where I felt envious of her. It came from a place of pain and insecurity, feeling as though my body had failed me in spite of my best effort, while she experienced such ease with minimal effort, or at least that is how it appeared to me…*

I am grateful for the messages of this dream. Things are not always as we see them, yet we serve as mirrors of each other. What we see in others often exist within us.

Envy as defined by Merriam-Webster is a *"painful or resentful awareness of an advantage enjoyed by another, joined with a desire to possess the same advantage."* Whenever we make unfair assumptions, we harbor feelings of envy. Being envious of the gifts in others often blinds us to the gifts that we hold within ourselves. Every person has a role in this intricate web of life. That role is specifically determined by the lived experiences, the challenges that serve to awaken our deeper gifts and the predilections and capacities one might have. Even if we share a similar ethnic background or the same family unit, we can still experience the world differently and so we might be called to serve in different ways.

Measuring our well-being by the well-being of others causes us to feel either superior or inadequate, neither of which serves anyone well. We cannot allow our health challenges to cause us to be resentful of the good health that others might appear to take for granted. Some of the deepest scars are invisible and pain wears many faces. As Pablo Picasso (*October 5, 1881 ~ April 8, 1973*) inquired, "Who sees the human face correctly: the photographer, the mirror, or the painter?" We cannot look at someone and conclude that we know everything that person might have lived in order to be as they are. Wellness can look different from one person to the next and can be achieved in various ways.

Harmony within is key to harmony without

Processing the emotions: May 22, 2020…*I close my eyes and move my awareness to my heart. I focus my thoughts on all the moments of peace and joy I have felt while in your presence. I feel immense* *gratitude for the memory of these moments. There have been many. I recall one of the most thoughtful gifts you ever gave to me. It was a heart-framed photo taken soon after I had given birth. Thank you for your thoughtfulness. I envision you smiling, healthy and safe. In this moment, I feel only gratitude. I send only love.*

This dream analysis also helps me in feeling more compassion towards those whose loss of livelihood is causing them to be more reactive during this time. The reality is that it takes much awareness and constant practice to release the patterns that no longer serve us. If the reactivity of others can threaten my sense of calm and peace, I must understand that they too are feeling threatened. Each one of us contribute to the harmony or disharmony of our environment.

As in music where harmony's role is to support the melody of a song, I choose to support the planetary vibration by doing whatever I can to maintain my sense of calm. This means that there are times where I might decide to love someone at a distance. I do not see this as disconnection; I see this as good self-care. And where there is love, there is always connection.

~ PRACTICE ~

Harmonizing the Heart, Mind and Body

Based on the teachings of Gregg Braden in his course, "Human by Design," I share this practice of heart-brain coherence to harmonize the body, mind and heart. This has become one of my favorite practices during this time.

- I invite you to close your eyes or soften your gaze, allowing your awareness to move to your heart.
- Place your hand, fingers or palm, at the center of your chest. Your hands are some of your most powerful tools for healing. Accept the guidance that will lead you in selecting this hand placement.
- Take a centering breath, inhaling for about a count of 5-4-3-2-1, exhale for a count of 5-4-3-2-1. Continue this cycle: B-r-e-a-t-h-e in and B-r-e-a-t-h-e out. Your breath connects you to your inmost being, your heart, your center, deepening your awareness of all that transcends this moment.
- Conjure up the feeling of gratitude, appreciation, care or compassion. This is done by calling to heart someone or something that easily give rise to one of these emotions.
- Hold the sensation of gratitude in your heart for a minimum of 3 minutes. Be open to what arises, a thought, a sensation, whatever arises. Adopt, if you will, the practice of making decisions

from this place—a reverent place of peace and calm that exists within—a place where you can return to again and again and as often as you choose.

The voice within says,

I resonate with the frequency of love, extending harmony around me as I experience harmony within. I listen, observe and accept my role in this intricate web of life. My melody is one of compassion. In gratitude, I send only love. I am a light of hope.

Chapter 6

Oneness

Dream Journal: May 24, 2020...The setting is inside what appears to be an auditorium. I am with a former roommate and we approach a makeshift altar to receive communion. I notice there are many conversations happening at the same time, and I begin to notice other familiar faces. The oddest element of this dream is that I have multiple toothbrushes in my pocket. There were at least five.

According to an online resource known as "Dream Moods," a dream of a toothbrush "suggests that you are feeling defensive about any criticism directed towards you. You are putting up a shield or barrier to protect yourself from potential hurt." Immediately after recording the details of this dream, I turn my chair to face the window, placing my hand on the center of my chest, connecting with my breath and bringing my awareness to my heart. It is easy to conjure up gratitude as I soften my gaze and notice the glistening of the sun like billions of distinct fireflies at the water's surface of the lake. I close my eyes and ask, *"What could these shields or barriers be?"*

The first thing that comes to mind is a face. It is a face I immediately recognize; someone I adored in my early teens and continue to hold in high regard even though he has encountered much ridicule. The words of a song he wrote begins to play in my mind and tears well up in my eyes. I spend a few moments watching the official video. More tears. The song is "Heal the World." The artist is Michael Jackson *(August 29, 1958 ~ June 25, 2009)*. And, as though this is all being orchestrated, about two hours later his name is mentioned in an online service. As a Memorial Day tribute, a mother and child deliver a heart-opening rendition of another of his songs. This one titled, "You Are Not Alone."

I return to my dream analysis after the service has ended. I have only ever attended public schools and universities so receiving communion in any auditorium has not been my physical reality. What comes to mind next is an actual conversation that occurred over twenty years ago. Mark is one of the recognizable persons in my dream. He is someone who had attended chiropractic school in the U.S. on a student visa. For some reason, I begin to recall a conversation we had one evening. We were at a dorm room gathering when he commented that I was the first black person he had ever had the opportunity of getting to know. I do not recall my response or where the conversation went after that.

And then it occurs me…I cannot speak about Oneness and not speak of all of the barriers to it. This dream was calling my attention to an incident from years ago. It was when I had accompanied my then fiancé to a wedding. The groom was one of his buddies from chiropractic school and the ceremony was held in a church with a traditional service where communion was offered. I approached the altar and held my palms to receive as I had often done in Anglican and Episcopal churches. I had even accompanied some of my college friends to Catholic mass. The Eucharistic minister looked at me, held the wafer up, but did not place the communion wafer into my palms. Assuming it was done differently in this church, I reached for it. "Are you Catholic?" she then asked. When I responded no, I was told "You can't receive." As I made my way back to my seat, trying to understand how she could have known I was not Catholic, I look around the church and I notice. I notice that I am the only person of color.

While discrimination should not be a welcomed guest in any house, especially a holy one, it seemed to have been present that day. For me, an altar is such a sacred place. I believe this is what made that experience so painful. I had hoped no one noticed, but my now husband did. "She is Christian," he said to her as he held his palms open and she placed his wafer without hesitation. Later at the reception, without me knowing, he approached the priest to discuss what had happened. I likely would have told him to forget about it, but this moment allowed me to see that he would not stand by and watch me be hurt; that I truly mattered. "Our lives begin to end the day we become silent about things that matter," said Dr. Martin Luther King, Jr. Yet, we often stay silent and put barriers in place to protect ourselves and our loved ones.

"How are you not angry?" a friend once asked. My default is not to anger when faced with racism, but to a crushing sadness. This sadness calls to mind all of my ancestors who chose death instead of a life of slavery that was being handed to them. I believe it is because of them that I was born with such a strong assertion to choose life no matter how hard it gets. This also calls to mind all of the lives lost to suicide when the injustices, the pain of a child's hunger, the pain of loneliness, the pain of unworthiness and all other sorrows have become just too much to bear. I choose life in honor of them as well.

We all filter the world though our earliest conditionings. Mental constructs regarding race, gender, social status, age, mental ability and physical health affect how we perceive and relate to one another. For some, it can be a constant awareness as a means of self-preservation. In the Caribbean, dark-skinned people are the predominant cultural group and often share multiple ethnicities, so I was less cognizant of racial disparities before coming to this country.

So, when have I experienced anger? When faced with a threat to my freedom or to the wellbeing of someone I love. These situations set off a fight response within me. I would never attack, but I will protect. I do understand the usefulness of anger and recognize its power to effect change when our innate powers are used for good. I also know that anger can be exhausting. It can be destructive. It can distort perception, so it is important to address the unhealthy aspects of this otherwise normal response to injustice, hatred and hypocrisy. Violence and retaliation are never valid solutions. They only serve to install more barriers to true healing. And as Indian lawyer Mahatma Gandhi *(October 2, 1869 ~ January 30, 1948)* would say, "An eye for an eye makes the whole world blind.

Oneness is love without barriers

"Your task is not to seek for love, but merely to seek and find all the

barriers within yourself that you have built against it," says Jalaluddin Rumi, 13th century Persian poet *(September 30, 1207 ~ December 17, 1273).* It did not take long to identify my barriers, especially the ones that pertain to my writing and earlier life experiences. Maybe take some time to identify your own. *Which barriers are you ready to dismantle and dispose of?*

1. There is a fear of not only feeling too exposed, but also of revealing too much that might cause members of my family to feel uncomfortable in any way that I can't possibly predict. The barrier: My ability to stay hidden. It would be so much more comfortable to remain unknown, unheard and unseen. Then the voice of Love says, *be seen, be heard, for you are already known in your Creator's heart, the oneness that intricately weaved you into existence; you, your brothers, your sisters and every other being."*

2. There is a fear of seeming foolish about the emphasis I place on coincidences. I remember when I first moved to the States and was teased incessantly for my choice of words like 'face basin' instead of bathroom sink, 'indicator' instead of turn signal, 'round-a-bout' instead of rotary. The barrier: My adaptability. I could easily adapt to what has been deemed most acceptable than be criticized. Then the voice of Love says, "*Be as you are. Before you were formed, you were declared sacred as is; you, your sisters, your brothers and every other being."*

3. There is a fear that this writing will not create the response I imagine; that others will know the details of my psyche and not care enough to sort through their own. Mission not accomplished. The barrier: Wanting to remain invulnerable. It would be easier to stop writing now or at least put it off until after I turn fifty when we magically stop caring about

what other people think. Then the voice of Love says, *you are being guided inasmuch as you were loved into existence and no thought has truly been your own."*

4. There is a fear of being attacked by fellow Christians as in Revelation 3:15-17 when the Spirit is speaking through John to the church in Laodicea. He says, *"I know your deeds, that you are neither cold nor hot. I wish you were either one or the other! So, because you are lukewarm, neither hot nor cold, I am about to spit you out of my mouth."* Yikes! The barrier: My ego questions and questions and questions, "Do I really want to put this out there?" The voice of Love simply says, *"You belong to love and always will."*

5. There is a fear of being seen as not Black enough, not Christian enough, not American enough or non-ambiguous enough when it comes to my ethnicity. *"I've never seen a black Webster,"* I was told when I was just a young girl. *"I've never seen a black person turn so red,"* a stranger remarked when I was a teen. *"You are Indian,"* another stranger once declared. *"Habla Espanol?"* Not enough to carry a conversation. And then I choose a career where *"You're not a real doctor"* and marry *"outside of your race." "Are you really an O'Malley?"* I was once asked when I handed a grocery clerk my credit card. And now, I worship in a church that someone recently described in an online forum as *"a feel-good church that's not really a religion."* When I shared the principles of the Unitarian Universalist Church, I was promptly asked, *"And where is God in all that?"* Love says; *empty your pockets of pain, limitation, apparent flaws and weakness for you were not just fearfully made; my child, you and all my beloved children are wholly and wonderfully made.*

Love, the voice of compassion, hope and wonder speaks through my innermost being, allowing me to dismantle my barriers and lay down my shields not in hopeless surrender, but in abidance with love. While I cannot say with absolute certainty that this is the voice of God that I hear, it speaks so lovingly that I hope it is. It is never authoritative or commanding. Maybe it knows I wouldn't listen if it was. Though inaudible, these words rise up in me, *"My love, you are always welcome at my table. Come as you are and you will always receive."*

Oneness is not sameness

Never again in history will there be another person exactly as I am or as you are. Even the life I gave birth to and have attempted to shape and mold has chosen her unique way of being. "You know how you always say kindness matters?" she attempted to make a point when she was about the age of nine; "Well I need to find my own words." And when she was ten, "Do you know that some people don't like people just because they are black…Well that's pretty dumb?" And at the age of fifteen when asked, "How do you feel about being both black and white?" She remarked in the way only a teenager could, "I like that I am neither." And yet, she wanted to attend protests in support of Black Lives Matter. I accompanied her to one, her dad accompanied her to another. And still with my guidance, I hope she continues to recognize that most police officers uphold their oath "to protect and serve."

Why is hatred part of our history? Is there an alternate Universe where every person is judged by character and not the color of their skin, the texture of their hair, the religion they practice or who they fall in love with? Or, are we being charged with creating this reality at this particular time in history?

What comes to mind is a jigsaw puzzle with billions of pieces. Imagine if we were all exactly the same. How would we ever find our unique place, a space that only one person could occupy so perfectly and feel a sense of *this is exactly where I belong*, right next to this one, in close proximity to these ones, giving rise to those ones, while making space for those ones over there, which are surrounded by other ones, giving form to yet other ones who then give rise to the ones beyond them, expanding and expanding until the picture becomes more complete and what continues to emerge could not be any more perfect than it is becoming. If every piece were to look exactly the same, where would we even start? None of us would ever really know our place, would we? The puzzle would forever remain incomplete.

Transcending Non-belonging

How do we begin to shift ways of thinking that no longer serve our highest evolution? Again, this can never be a once and done practice. Like an onion, there are always layers no matter which way you choose to cut into it. So, begin with whatever arises. When I look back at the wedding incident, this moment occurred during a time when I held within me the need to fit in, adapt to my current surroundings and remain somewhat camouflaged. Even at school, when professors publicly commended my writing, I felt uncomfortable and wanted to hide. That sense of non-belonging is deeply rooted as I share about in Chapter 4. I have also had various dreams of hiding in order to remain safe. I can recall wartime images and being in foreign lands, hearing unrecognizable languages. Could these simply have been movie scenes that my creative brain held on to and manipulated while I slept? Who knows? I remain open to all possibility.

I believe that most people can grow beyond limited beliefs if we allow them to become better versions of themselves rather than judge them by a single incident or period of time. Just because you have a bad experience at the dentist does not mean you should never again get your teeth cleaned professionally. If we persist in judging someone by a past action, we miss the opportunities to witness the beauty of change and evolution. Who knows? Maybe life has offered her an opportunity to see things differently. Wherever she is, I wish her well.

Hold on to what is essential in you

I am who I am because of everything that I have lived. I will also do my best to respect societal standards and grow with changing times, while recognizing that there are some aspects of myself that are essential to who I am. Many teachings focus on releasing what no longer serves. What about everything else that makes us all that we are? Here are some aspects of myself that I have come to embrace and will continue to hold on to. In sharing them, I hope they will inspire you to consider what you intend to hold on to as you grow and evolve. Interspersed are messages from a Pueblo blessing that was timely shared (May 25, 2020).

1. I have a need to feel connected to the ground: Having grown up on an island, dirt and rocky surfaces will always feel more comfortable to my feet than shoes. I have been known to walk around my neighborhood without shoes. Truth be told, I would be without shoes more often than not if I could avoid calling attention to myself. It just feels good.

Hold on to what is good, even if it is a handful of dirt.

2. I must decipher what is true for me: Reading scripture was my grandmother's *thing* and I feel closest to her whenever I read and hear certain verses and hymns. Yet, not all of scripture rings true for me. I do not see myself as a *lukewarm* Christian. I am a follower of Christ's teachings. His message has always been to be love and show compassion.

Hold on to what you believe, even if it is a tree that stands by itself.

3. I will remain curious with varied interests: My desk will never remain neat and orderly no matter how diligent I am because that is not how my brain is wired or how my life is designed. No, I cannot be focused on just one thing. I even enjoy reading more than one book at a time. I will finish what I start, but in my own time unless I have committed otherwise.

Hold on to what you must do, even if it is a long way from here.

4. I will resist technology: A notebook and pen were my first loves and will always be my favorite medium no matter how much more efficient technology becomes. Yes, it might be easier and quicker to cut and paste thoughts and ideas into a computer program but forming words with a pen in hand breathes life into my soul.

Hold on to life, even if it is easier to let go.

5. I need to be free: I do not take for granted the magnitude of all that my ancestors endured so that I might live free. Each time I choose aliveness instead of obligation, it is in part out of respect for their efforts. Each time I choose compassion instead of ridicule, I do so with them in

mind. They were not all-knowing people and I imagine they made their share of mistakes, but they learned what was needed for their survival, allowing me to be here. Each time I choose hope over anguish, I do so in honor of them. Yes, I will remember that I am a descendent of slaves and immigrants. I will also remember that I am a descendent of great physicians and healers, warriors and innovators. I will continue to hold their hands in mine as I move about this physical world, accepting their support and guidance from the world of Spirit.

Hold on to my hand, even if I have gone away from you.

What is on your list of *non-negotiables*? When do you feel closest to the people you have loved and lost?

It is not rejection when you are being led elsewhere

In the Anglican church we recite the Nicene Creed that reads, *"I believe in one, holy, catholic and apostolic Church."* I have repeated these words so often that it did not occur to me that I could not receive communion in a Catholic church. *They are similar but not the same*, the priest explained to my husband. My husband, on the other hand, grew up in an Irish Catholic family, so I had a fleeting thought of converting to Catholicism. I might have if not for that incident. Our firstborn daughter was christened in the Catholic church. Part of the motivation was to ensure that she would never be turned away from any altar. But the more I thought about it, the more certain I became that my place was not in a church community where all were not welcomed to receive the Eucharist.

A single experience does not have to define your life or shape your future. However, some instances allow us to recognize that *maybe this is not really where I belong.* I still appreciate Catholic rituals. I attend family weddings, funerals and other ceremonies where I remain seated at the Eucharist. During this time, I focus my awareness on the Christ within me and I am nourished in His presence. And if our daughter ever wants to practice Catholicism, she can still choose that for herself.

As previously shared in Chapter 2, a chance conversation in a grocery store led me to a different community. That date was Sunday, June 10, 2007. I was buying flowers in memory of our second daughter who had passed hours after birth one year earlier, when a stranger engaged me in conversation. She was also getting flowers in memory of her late husband. She shared other details of her life and I politely listened. About twenty minutes later, she mentioned St. Andrew's, a nearby Episcopal Church where she attended. What she could not have known is that I was feeling the need to find a church community and while I had not begun to actively search, just days prior I did pray for guidance. This woman who I would never see again was an answer to my prayer.

And now thirteen years later, St. Andrew's no longer exists as it was, merging with another small parish, making a new home in another building. You know how people say it is not about the building, that a church is the people. Yes, this is true, but there was also something about that building. I felt it every time I walked in. And yes, the people. I love them, always. While I do visit from time to time, I have found another community that feels most aligned with where I am in my life and my spiritual fulfillment. Not knowing anything about the Unitarian Universalist (UU) Church, I only attended at the invitation of a friend to hear her husband sing in the choir. What was supposed to be a one-time visit led me to discover yet another place that feels like home, with another circle of people who have become my extended family. Likewise, my daughter has met some great friends. *"Thank you for forcing me to join the youth group,"* she said with sincerity one day on our way to a friend's dance recital. They may not have met otherwise.

In Oneness, you are not alone

Hearing Michael Jackson's *"You are not alone"* sung by mother and child was a reminder that we are forever tied to that from which we came. Studies reveal that a woman carries within her all of the *eggs* she will ever produce while in her mother's womb. This means that my grandmother carried me within her, and her grandmother carried her just as your grandmother carried you. Similarly, we share this connection with the land and the sea. "We are tied to the ocean. And when we go back to the sea, whether it is to sail or to watch it, we are going back from whence we came," declared President John F. Kennedy (*May 29, 1917 ~ November 22, 1963*). We are one with the oceans and the lands, the skies and the stars. We belong to the seas and the lands. We belong to each other.

We are never alone especially in those moments when we might feel most alone. Even in grief, we are being initiated into something new. We are not alone in aligning with integrity and intention. Rather, intention seeks us out and somehow finds us. We are not alone in seeking purpose and meaning. We are held. We are supported. We are guided. We are loved along the way no matter how far away we get from where we have yet to go.

You belong to love

Remember your roots. You originated from Love no matter how you came to exist in this physical form. You were created as you are for a purpose that only you can fulfill. You belong to no one and yet you belong to all. You are Love's child, Love's flesh and blood. You are Love's promise and Love's divine assignment. You belong to Love, always.

~ PRACTICE ~

Adding Your Drop into the Ocean of Oneness

This ritual is based on the water ceremony that occurs every September in the Unitarian Universalist Church. Members are invited to bring a small amount of water from a place that is special to them. During the service, all of the waters are placed into one container. This water is used throughout the year in other ceremonies. Similarly, this practice invites you to add your hopes, dreams and intentions to the Ocean of Oneness.

     Fill a small container with water and place this water on your altar or another place in your home where it is easily accessible. Each morning for about a week, hold this container in your hands for just a few moments, thinking about your hopes and dreams and intentions for your day, your community and the world. Each evening as you consider the smallest blessings of the day and experience a sense of gratitude, hold this container as though you can transmit this feeling to everything you touch. At the end of the week, find a place to empty your container into a larger source of water somewhere in your community. It can be added to a stream, a lake, a pond. It can be used to water a plant somewhere in your neighborhood or community park. As Mother Teresa would say, "…we can do small things with great love."

The voice within says,

Insight: Embracing Life, Discovering Beauty, Grace and True Purpose

I am Love's child, Love's promise and Love's divine assignment. I belong to Love.

Chapter 7

Purpose

There are no accidents in an intelligent universe, so all the dark times, accidents, illnesses and broken dreams were part of your spiritual advancement…honor them, and then transform them in your own way.
~Dr. Wayne Dyer

On May 8th, 2019, I walked away from a car accident with only minor aches and stiffness although my RAV4 had to be towed from the scene and determined to be a total loss. When the young man approached my window to say, "I'm sorry, I only looked away for a..." I took a long breath. I did not want to say "It's okay" because in that moment, it did not feel okay. My heart was racing, my head was hurting, and I was unsure of what to do next. I could have easily been dismissive of his apology. Instead, by taking that one breath I was able to ask, "Are you okay?" He said he was and continued to apologize repeatedly until I found myself saying, 'It's okay, no one is seriously hurt, it's okay." Within minutes, an officer arrived at the scene, assisted with the exchange of information and called for the tow truck. This police officer happened to be Krista's brother-in-law.

There are no accidents

Hours later, through an unusual set of circumstances, I learn that this same young man had experienced a tragic loss years before and the person he had lost would have celebrated a birthday right around this time. I was grateful I had shown compassion in that moment. Just maybe he needed to hear on that particular day that everything would be okay. I said a prayer for him and his family, thinking this was the ultimate reason for this collision.

Two days prior to this accident, I had a dream of walking about the streets of a large city much like New York City. It was a lucid dream; the type of dream where you have the awareness that this cannot possibly be happening, but it is. You can feel, you can hear, you can read written words and relate to an unfamiliar environment. Yet you somehow know this is all a dream.

> Dream Journal: May 6, 2019...*There is a street sign. It feels important that I remember the name of this street when I wake up. I observe it for a while, committing it to memory. I walk a little way before entering a small market. I enter, walking around a display of vegetables. I then turn right and then walk straight ahead. There seated in the aisle is a young man. He is not someone I know. He is dressed in all white. He stands, extends his hand to greet me. He tells me his name. I wake up.*

As much as I try, I cannot recall the name of the street although I was intentional about committing it to memory. I can remember entering the market, turning to the right and walking towards the young man. I can recall his face, his physical features, and his mannerisms. He stands, leans forward a bit, offers me his hand and says, "My name is…" I go on the internet and I search. I search street names to see if something would jog my memory; Nothing. I then search the name that was given to me in my dream. Nothing draws my attention.

So, imagine my surprise the day after the accident when I am handed a driver's license for identification purposes, bearing not only the uncommon name that was given to me in my dream, but the day of birth is May 6th. May 6th is not only the date of my recent dream, but it is also the birthday of the young man's relative who had passed on years ago; the one from the accident. And if that wasn't enough, what I thought was a most unusual name appeared in different ways again and yet again in a matter of days.

The following Monday, I woke up with the thought to search the name that kept reappearing combined with the surname of the young man from the accident. Within a matter of seconds, I was looking at a photo of the young man from my dream and his Facebook page showed that he is very much alive. It was not only his face but the accuracy of his mannerisms that was so distinct. I do not know this man. I am quite certain that our paths have never crossed as we live many miles away. So how could this happen? I understand how I'm able to dream of my grandparents and other loved ones, those who have passed on and those who are still here. I understand how I can dream of people such as Dr. Dyer even before he transitioned although we never met in person. I even get how I can dream of someone I never knew in life, but having seen a photo of her, I understand how her essence and the image of her face can enter my dreams. But how could I dream of a total stranger who exists in present time reality and most importantly, why?

After the shock dissipated, I went on to discover that he is a musician. I figured I could listen to some of his music while walking my dog that morning. One song called to mind a spiritual text, *Christ in You*, written by Joseph Benner, but published anonymously in 1919. At that time, this book had been on my bookshelf for about a year, a purchase I had made on Amazon. I decided to just open this book and see where I would land. My eyes immediately fell upon these words found on page 29 in a lesson titled, *He That Hath Seen Me, Hath Seen the Father*:

> *"...men and women from time to time have made this discovery...They are no longer pilgrims and strangers, but children in the Father's home...There is no separation... To enter heaven is to become lifted into a larger consciousness of God...There is no parting, but only greater unity, No belief in distance and space is possible on the spiritual plane."*

In Spirit, we are not strangers

This seemed to provide an explanation for what had occurred in my recent dream. Somehow, I had stepped into a larger consciousness where I could experience greater unity and recognize that we are not complete strangers. This is not the first lucid dream I have had. But it was the first instance where someone unknown to me was clearly aware of my presence and interacted with me in such an obvious way. This then led me to take a closer look at Joseph Benner's other work, *The Impersonal Life*. I felt as though I had gotten a glimpse of what this title actually meant; *Impersonal* is that which exists beyond the personality; beyond character, beyond gender, race, ethnicity, religion and creed.

Transcending Powerlessness

On the morning of May 6, 2019, I stopped at the mailbox on the way to bringing my daughter and niece to school. This was a Monday morning and it occurred to me that I had not checked the mail since Friday. There was an envelope from the Department of Motor Vehicles. As soon as I was parked at the office, I opened it to find that my car registration was cancelled due to non-payment of insurance. Typically, I pay our insurance annually, one payment and then I do not have to think about it for another year. Somehow, I missed the payment and now realize I had driven uninsured and without a valid registration that morning. I immediately inform my husband, who calls our local insurance agent and he gets right on it. By the end of the day, all is well.

I share these details for two reasons. First, had our insurance not been temporarily cancelled, I would not have learned the details surrounding the young man's father. Also, after realizing I had driven without insurance, I did think to myself, *what if I had been involved in an accident on my way to school or the office this morning.* It was a fleeting thought and I was grateful that I had stopped to quickly get the mail and had taken the time to open that envelope before work and not at the end of my workday. This reminds me of a message in the first chapter of *You Can Create an Exceptional Life* written by authors Louise Hay and Cheryl Richardson. *Answer the phone and open the mail* is the message with the overarching message being, "Everything happens in the perfect-time-space sequence." I believe this to be true. Somehow, it all falls into place, often with the help of persons who show up at just the right moment, at a thrift store, a gas station or at a book signing. It might not always be immediate or in the way we would expect, but somehow we end up being okay. At times, we end up even better than okay.

The power of intention will find you

Transcending powerlessness is about realizing that we do not have to have such a firm grip on a desired outcome. English author Douglas Adams *(March 11, 1952 ~ May 11, 2001)* made this observation: "I may not have gone where I intended to go, but I think I have ended up where I intended to be." This is also the highlighted message in my first book, Messages *from Within, Finding Meaning in Your Life Experiences*. It is neither the book I set out to write nor one I could easily promote to others. I cried many tears through the process of writing it and so have many readers. One person graciously likened it to "a cleansing of the soul." Another shared that she could not finish it. I understand. Still, I have been incredibly humbled by the grace that has allowed me to bear witness to how it has allowed for healing in others, both men and women.

"Thank you," she says, while the tears are pouring from her eyes. She grabs me by the shoulders. Today was to be her final visit with me. I was running behind schedule and she had picked up a copy of my book and started reading. *But you're sobbing, why are you thanking me*, I did not have to ask because she explained right there in front of my office manager and another patient. "I haven't been able to cry in eleven years. My husband died and I stopped being able to cry." She continued to explain that she had tried medication and therapy. Her doctors eventually told her not to worry about it.

My second book, *Messages from Children and What They Can Teach Grownups* was born out of the twelfth chapter of my first book. Chapter 12, titled, *Through the Eyes of a Child,"* was based on the poem by Lebanese-American poet, Kahlil Gibran *(January 6, 1883 ~ April 10, 1931)*, "Your children are not your children," he offers in *The Prophet*. My intention with this book was to share encouraging messages from children as well as from my own childhood experiences, replacing non-affirming messages with more affirming ones. Parents and grandparents were my intended audience. Aside from that, I could not predict how readers would respond.

Your life is your purpose

"Tell your wife I said thank you," my husband shared as he relayed the message. This time it was one of his patients on a return visit. This man had purchased a copy of my second book and apparently was moved by the first chapter, "Be Happy Now." Here is what set the stage for this message:

> "Mom, I don't think I'm going to college because I feel like I'm going to peak too soon and I will want to do other things." We were in the car and like the start of many of our conversations, this was completely unexpected.

"What do you mean by peak to soon?"

"Well...it's just that I might want to try other things."

"Well you're eight and feelings change. Besides, you really don't have to think about that right now..."

I went on to say that we do not have to have our entire lives mapped out. We can make plans and set goals. We can also allow things to unfold. I also pointed out that being happy now is really about this moment and who you choose to share it with. As my husband explained, this man was moved to reach out to his son after reading this message. They were estranged because of his son's decision not to attend college. This phone call led to reconciliation.

Your purpose is not any one achievement. It is all that you are and all that you are still becoming. It is in every interaction you have, every dream shared, every creation you have brought forth and everything you will ever bring forth. You are your purpose. Your life is your purpose. If you are moved to create something, you owe it to yourself to just see where it goes. You do not have to know the lesson, the message or what happens next. You just have to *answer the phone and open the mail* and do your best to pay your bills on time.

Be patient with yourself

Whether it is a car accident, a slip and fall or an illness, unforeseen or chronic, physical pain or mental anguish, these circumstances challenge our ability to find meaning and purpose in moments that appear to be most void of purpose. How do you focus on anything else when you are hurting? How do you live your relationships well? How do you explore creativity when the cells and tissues in your body alert you to your limitations and deficiencies?

Pain is a signal, calling our attention to what needs our immediate focus and care. We cannot ignore it, deny it or simply wish it away. Pain must be listened to and heard, observed, explored and tended to. Painful conditions require patience and compassion, not inner our outer criticism. A less-abled body or a less-abled mind requires comfort and nourishment, not resentment. You may not have had any control over the onset of illness or painful injury. Yet, from this moment forward, you can choose to be patient with yourself.

You can choose whatever is comforting, helpful or provides hope. You can allow yourself to be comforted. You can choose whatever relieves the pain without causing further harm. You can notice the joy and the beauty that show up as a butterfly or a hummingbird or in the eyes of a loved one. You can choose to keep in mind that pain does not diminish the essence of who you are. It might cause you to forget in a moment of anger and frustration. That is perfectly normal. And then, come right back to yourself. You are your purpose. Your life is your purpose. Breathe, take a nap, do whatever you can in this moment. *This too shall pass.*

Transcending powerlessness is also about realizing that while there is much beyond our control, there are still choices we can make. Prayers are not always answered as we prayed them, yet we can grow in acceptance of what is, take inspired actions and allow for the emergence of something meaningful and purposeful. As far as I know, we cannot yet grow a new arm or a new lung, but we can adapt and use available innovations that allow us to function beyond our limitations. We cannot trade in our genes for better ones, but we can adopt habits that allow for the healthiest expression of this body and this mind. We cannot live this life and not be vulnerable to loss, to pain, to sorrow, to fear, but we can heal and choose life and hope and love, and be of service to humankind.

What is your song?

As Maya Angelou would say, "A bird does not sing because it has an answer, it sings because it has a song." Likewise, we are here to experience all that this life has to offer; The joys, the sorrows and everything in between. We live this life because this is *the one* we have been given. This is the one to be lived. Sometimes they are no easy answers. Tragedy might serve a greater purpose; nevertheless, it is still painful. What we do with that pain then becomes our song. Songs express the fullness of our experiences. We might borrow melodies from those who came before us. Or, we might write entirely different lyrics. No matter what, we get to decide how our song will be sung.

My grandmother's song was *Amazing Grace*. She could often be heard humming or singing this and other hymns. She even woke up singing the one time she endured surgery. My song would be a compilation of lyrics and melodies, my grandmother's song, *Blue Boat Home* as sung by Peter Mayer, India Arie's *I Am Light*, Michael Jackson's *Heal the World* and *Three Little Birds* by Bob Marley. What are the lyrics of your song?

~ PRACTICE ~

Deciding How Your Song Will Be Sung

Light a candle and place it before you. Assume a comfortable position on a chair or on the floor. Imagine you are sitting around a campfire with your ancestors; those who have done their healing work and are now capable of supporting you and the highest good of all. Know that you are safe and guarded in this moment, surrounded and held by unconditional love. Rest your hands with your palms up and be open to receiving. Bring your attention to the candle. Let the flame enchant and empower you. What songs did your ancestors sing? How will your song be sung?

The voice within says,

As I live and breathe and move through each moment, I use my powers for good. I honor this body and this mind. My voice is my instrument of hope. My song is of loss and discovery, grief and of wonder, and great thanksgiving.

Insight: Embracing Life, Discovering Beauty, Grace and True Purpose

Chapter 8

Expression

Kintsukuroi, also known as Kintsugi is the Japanese art of repairing pottery with gold, silver or platinum lacquer with the understanding that the broken piece is part of the history, rather than something to be disguised. Each crack is viewed as a unique expression of the whole. Why then do we attempt to deny and disguise the aspects of ourselves that are deemed unacceptable by others? "Seared with scars," wrote Kahlil Gibran to describe those persons who have become more solid in themselves because of all they have lived.

Explore the callings of your heart

Early in 2013, attempting to make sense of my dream experiences, I began reading about some of the mystics, Meister Eckhart, Francis of Assisi, Julian of Norwich, Mother Teresa and St. Teresa of Avila. Recently, I have been drawn again to Julian of Norwich. Just this morning (May 29, 2020), I began a 30-day practice with a little book titled *"All Will Be Well: 30 Days with a Great Spiritual Teacher."* The first prayer speaks of a hazelnut in the palm of her hand. The image of the hazelnut is symbolic for the incidents that seem as small and as insignificant as the hazelnut.

I wondered if I might stumble upon a *hazelnut* at some point today. Well I did. Moments ago, I discovered the date when Julian of Norwich, less commonly known as Mother Julian received her series of visions that led to the writing of *Revelations of Divine Love*. It was on May 8, 1373. Just yesterday, I wrote about the car accident occurring on May 8, 2019 that set me back upon the path of writing this book. And May 8th continues to catch my attention. I am still awed by the synchronicity that…I was about to say follows…but it feels more so that it leads, leaving behind shiny marbles along the way for us to discover.

This aligns with more recent thoughts. I share in Chapter 2 about the recurrence of April 10th, an auspicious date since childhood. I couldn't help but notice throughout this writing that three beloved spiritual teachers transitioned from this Earth on this day: Kahlil Gibran, April 10, 1931; Pierre Teilhard de Chardin, April 10, 1955; Howard Washington Thurman, April 10, 1981. Now as I look back through earlier journals, some pretty interesting happenings have also occurred during the Month of May. We often hear that the *veil between worlds* thins in autumn, nearing the end of October. I wonder if this also happens during the month of May.

Transcending Self-Doubt

In a world where the loudest and most controversial voices often draw the most attention, it requires diligence to connect to your truest feelings and innermost voice. While our bodily sensations are informative, our deepest awareness also has much wisdom to share. We doubt ourselves when we have not yet mastered the art of listening to our inner being. We doubt ourselves when we choose to fill potential space with something to do and not enough quiet in order to truly hear. Mantras help us to move beyond the thinking mind. Prayer shifts responsibility from the ego to a greater Source of power. Still, it is when we become immersed in quiet and we listen, our innermost wisdom begins to emerge. From this inner spaciousness we discover that everything, even doubt, can be useful in some way.

The usefulness of doubt

Did you ever consider that every seed of doubt allows for a more discerning heart? This question arose one starlit evening as I walked my dog. These were the thoughts that followed when I sat down to write:

> Journal entry: December 13, 2016...*Why isn't our faith, trust, belief in a force greater than ourselves enough to protect, shield, save us from the unpleasant realities that do exist?*
>
> *And through the silence of this night, it is as though I hear what sounds like Gil's voice, coming from within.*
>
> *"Did you ever consider that God desires for each of you to believe in yourselves inasmuch as you place your trust in the Father?*
>
> *"Did you ever consider that every seed of self-doubt allows for a more discerning heart?*
>
> *That every apparent misdirection or misstep*

holds the possibility of an even greater self-discovery...

That every feeling of angst just might be a call for greater attention to your inner world first, and then to the world around you...

That every healing you experience unveils a deeper strength...

That every moment of despair inspires greater hope in some way?

Did you ever consider that maybe Christ did not come to save, shield, protect you or anyone else? That he traveled this earth just as you and me... trying to find his way...

And when he saw the hurt and suffering caused and endured by his brothers and sisters, he then chose to be a force for good...a voice of love and compassion...a healing presence...

Maybe when he said, "Come and follow me," He may not have meant...do as I do...

But rather, to take the path that is most dear to your heart...

To follow the calling of your inner being...

To love in the way that the deepest part of you is

able to love…

*To serve in the way that is most honoring of who
you are.*

Where were these words coming from? Gil is a priest I met at *Terre Nouvelle* in Canada and I once watched a video here he asked us to consider that "God wants us to believe in ourselves as much as we believed in him." These are the only words I recall from that video. I had forgotten these words until I was looking at past journals. In this same journal May 8th is written in the top margin with no explanation. This journal is from 2016.

Maybe our faith, trust and belief in God does not feel like enough until we learn to trust and believe in our own deepest experience; until we each recognize that no one can give to the world exactly what you or I have to give. A sense of doubt provides caution to wait just a bit longer. Allow more time to consider all the options, those present and those yet to be revealed. An idea might require more nurturing, more study, more growth. Not every tree's blossoms will bear fruit," a friend once shared. When I looked up the origin of this quote, I learned it is a Mauritanian proverb. Mauritania is an independent county in Northwest Africa, best described as barren and beautiful. Its name calls to mind a dream from the other night.

> Dream Journal…May 28, 2020…*I'm on an archaeological expedition of some sort. A group of us come upon an artifact of value. It becomes evident that I am not the one in charge when I ask permission to obtain a sample of some sort. Permission is granted.*

I do not recall any additional details at the moment. I cannot call to mind any of the faces of my fellow explorers. I do not know the location, country or site of this supposed expedition. I have not watched television in days. So where did this dream come from? I have no idea, but it felt important to share.

Permission granted...

Societal norms often caution us not to say or do or be anything that might provoke ridicule or upset. However, we do not all experience the world in the same way. As spoken by a former American President, "...we are a nation of Christians and Muslims, Jews and Hindus— and nonbelievers..." He referred to this as "our patchwork heritage," declaring it to be a strength rather than a weakness. I agree. No matter our religious ideation, we all serve something beyond ourselves. We are a patchwork of ancient teachings and modern findings. We are a patchwork of scientific methodology and spiritual phenomena. As Robin Williams (July 21, 1951 ~ August 11, 2014) in his role as *Patch Adams* said, "we're all just trying to find our way home." By sharing what is true for us, we grant others permission to express what is true for them. An open exchange is how we learn, grow and find our way.

Say everything, my friend, author of *Waiting for Grace* and psychic medium, Caroline Zani would say. She facilitates monthly groups for those wanting to share about their intuitive experiences. I spoke about my dream that preceded the May 8th car accident and the synchronicities that followed in our group one evening, which prompted a newcomer to share that she had experienced a miscarriage that same day. She openly expressed her feelings and reflections surrounding this loss. Although she had not planned to share such intimate details of her life in a group of mostly strangers, she soon realized that this was a place where she could say anything.

If you are seeking permission to be as you are, this could be the reason you were guided to this book. It is important that we each speak our thoughts and feelings out loud and with compassion as opposed to yelling at each other. This is how we connect, understand and evolve. Not everyone will respond the way you might hope and that too is okay. As Dr. Wayne Dyer would say, "What other people think of you is none of your business."

Creative minds...

Recently, my husband recounted a childhood memory of one his friends. This friend was known for being that witty kid who could make even the most astute teacher erupt into uncontrollable laughter. My husband relayed this story of his friend having such difficulty with a set of math equations one day. All of them, he had gotten wrong. *Here is the problem,* the teacher explained. She recognized that every time he arrived at the same step in solving the equation, he would do the complete reverse of what he was supposed to. *Oh I get it,* his childhood friend exclaimed. *Every time I think to do it this way, I should do it the exact opposite and it will be right.* While this worked in his case, imagine trying to live your life in that way. Doing or being the complete opposite of how you are wired in order for it to be viewed as the *right* way. Of course, there are certain rules and regulations that allow us to stop, proceed with caution, compromise and allow for safety and order that constitute our ability to co-exist. And then, they are other expectations that only hinder, hurt and humiliate.

While learning something new builds neural connections in the brain, we do not all learn at the same pace and in the same way. When we expect children to conform simply because *this is the way it has always been done*, we risk hindering their creative expression. When we constantly tell them how to think and what to see, we risk witnessing the purity of how they see the world. Our littlest minds can often speak the greatest wisdom.

Laugh, even at yourself

One of my sisters recently shared with my daughter about some of my earlier accomplishments—valedictorian, spelling bee champion, pageant winner and yes, my *Messy Desk Award*. Of course, my daughter harped on the Messy Desk Award, "That still fits," I heard her say. When I graduated from chiropractic school, my mom had given me a binder that contained every award I had ever received. I burnt my *Messy Desk Award* quite ceremoniously years ago. I made the mistake of sharing this fact with my daughter in the presence of my husband. They looked at my desk, then at each other and I knew what was coming next. "It didn't work," one of them teased. "You must not have done Qigong afterwards," one of them added. We all shared a good laugh at my expense.

I was in the fifth grade when my teacher whom I still adored thought it was a good idea. I can sincerely laugh about it now, but my younger self managed to hide my humiliation behind a smile. That day I also received the *Super Scientist Award* and was voted by my classmates as *Most Studious*. These were some of the same kids who would call me names because I would always be first to finish those speed math worksheets. What my classmates never realized is that I promptly completed the work required of me, so that I could get to the work that inspired me. I would use my *free* time to write poetry, short stories, songs. So yes, my desk had more paper then anyone else's.

And yes, it still fits. Even today, there are several different journals and books on my desk, with mail and tax documents in the mix. There are certain tasks I must attend to, alongside my writing. I do the best to manage both the best I can.

Our outer environment mirrors our inner one

For a few weeks, courtesy of the pandemic, my desk was almost immaculate. It was one of the things I could easily control. Now, slowly I see it inching towards *organized chaos*. Somehow, I seem to maintain a general idea of where to search for something I presently need. My desk has always been an obvious expression of my life. I would not define it as truly chaotic, just trying to juggle all aspects of myself and my varied interests. In chiropractic school, my husband once left me a note, "I thought about cleaning up your place, but then I came to my senses." Even then I found time to journal and write creatively, while juggling classes, tutoring Biochemistry and attending my duties as Resident Assistant of one of the dorm buildings. I speak about creating balance often and yet I am nowhere close to mastering it. Everything I am involved in feels essential in my life. The thought occurs that maybe balance is less about even distribution and more about creating the space for it all. When your attention is toward a friend in need one day and then back to writing a book the next, that is balance.

While some writers might require a tidy writing space, I manage to create amidst the mess. Maybe it is about comfort because this is how I have always been, at least since the fifth grade. Maybe it is something that requires more diligence. Or maybe it is just another aspect of me that I have come to embrace. I also recognize the ease of everything having its place. I also enjoy cleaning and organizing when time permits. It is just that I enjoy other things more. I have found I am most tidy and organized when I am either procrastinating or needing to move the energy of frustration. *Why not hire someone*, multiple people have asked. Hmm…the first answer is that it keeps my hands busy when I wish to listen to a book on *Audible* or tune into a Summit where I can hear from various people on various topics. When we were younger, I used to pay my sister to do the chores so I could read and write. There is also the satisfaction that comes with organizing and cleaning whenever the inspiration occurs or when I need to dispel sensations of anger and frustration. So, my mess serves a purpose in some way.

What does your current environment say about how you are currently living? Who or what makes your days most enjoyable and meaningful?

What will your legacy be?

A man in his eighth decade of life once lamented that his main regret about not having any children is that he will never know the joys of having grandchildren. He looked to the rock in his hand that he had brought into the session with him. "Unlike this rock that has always been and will always be here," he said. "There will be no one to continue my legacy. When I'm gone, I'm gone." I was surprised to hear this from such an incredible teacher, a museum enthusiast, who also served as a professor and devoted his life in service to God. I assured him that I for one will never forget him. I dedicate the following practice to him.

~ PRACTICE ~

Painted Rock Meditation

Find a rock upon your path and using whatever materials you choose; add whatever color you choose to this rock. Keep the practice of Kintsukuroi in mind whether you choose to add gold or silver, red or yellow. Place this rock in your garden, outside your front door or gift it a friend. Recognize that your legacy is what is left behind in the hearts of those you have touched regardless of relational ties.

The voice within says,

I see the Divine in all things and in all beings. I am an expression of Divine love. My legacy will be love.

Chapter 9

Genius

"Boldness has genius, power and magic in it."

~Johann Wolfgang von Goethe

(August 28, 1749~ March 22, 1832)

When I shared in one of my circles of women of how the outline for this book appeared, one of the women said it reminded her of a story told by Elizabeth Gilbert in her book, *Big Magic*. This was early in March 2020. Just weeks ago, another friend mentioned the same book and so I decided to purchase it on *Audible*. In another astonishing example of synchronicity, I listened to Elizabeth Gilbert speak of inspiration and creative ideas as *disembodied consciousness* seeking a willing participant to bring them into the world. She described genius as an external creative power, a view that immediately resonated with me.

In ancient times, the Romans saw *genius* as a guardian spirit that provided inspiration or guidance. A genius would offer visions to multiple people at the same time. Instead of being viewed as *the* genius or mastermind, a person was seen as having a genius, allowing them to be less egocentric and more delighted for the inspiration bestowed upon them. This is precisely how I felt about the outline for this book, as though I was being presented with the honor of bringing forth a healing guide, revealing that we are more connected than we might realize. When I wrote the word 'genius' for the G- in grace, I still recall how I paused and looked at the word. It was in that moment I knew that this writing was beyond my rational mind.

Be aware of comparisons

In its early stages, I found myself comparing this writing to that of others. *What could I possibly say that has not already been said, especially about courage?* Begin with courage was the guidance I kept receiving. *Where would I fit in when there are already so many established writers sharing similar themes and the media seems to focus on the loudest, most controversial voices?*

I cannot say for certain how this writing might have evolved had it not been for the car accident in May 2019 and the synchronicities that followed. I did not want to write a book to say essentially what has already been said. "Most things have already been done," Elizabeth Gilbert offers, "but they have not yet been done by you." Message received, thank you.

When we compare ourselves, we risk losing sight of all that we are and the contributions we can make to our evolving world. We risk our authenticity when we attempt to abide by the standards of others. There is also a risk to our integrity as illustrated in one of my favorite fables, *The Emperor's Seed.*

> *There was an Emperor from China who had no children, but he needed to select a successor. Children from across the kingdom came to the palace. He gave them all a seed and they were instructed to go home to their villages, plant the seed in a pot and tend to it for a year. The Emperor would then judge their efforts and choose his successor.*
>
> *Once a week, the children of the village would gather to compare their plants. After a few weeks, there were signs of life in all the pots except for one that belonged to a young boy named Ling. The weeks passed and Ling continued to water his pot every day.*
>
> *After a few months, some of the pots had flowers and some had leafy shrubs. Ling still had nothing growing in his pot. The other children made fun of him. Ling continued to water his pot every day.*
>
> *A year passed and it was time to return to the palace to show what had*

grown and decide on the new heir. Ling was anxious as his pot still showed no signs of life. "What if they mock me? They won't know that I've watered it every day, they'll think that I'm lazy."

Ling's mother explained that whatever the consequences were, he had to return and show the Emperor his barren pot. By now, some of the plants were magnificent and the children were wondering which one the Emperor would choose. Ling was embarrassed as other children scoffed at his lifeless pot.

The Emperor came and started to make his way through the crowd, looking at the many impressive trees, shrubs and flowers on display.

Then the Emperor came to Ling.

"What happened here?" He asked.

"I watered the pot every day, but nothing ever grew." Ling stated nervously.

After a few hours, the Emperor finally finished his assessment.

"Clearly, some of you desperately want to be Emperor and would do anything to make that happen, but there is one boy that has come to me with nothing. Ling, come here please."

"Oh no," thought Ling. He slowly made his way to the front of the group, holding his barren pot.

The Emperor held up the pot for all to see and the other children laughed. Then the Emperor continued, "A year ago, I gave you all a seed. I told you to go away, plant the seed and return with your plant. The seeds that I gave you all were boiled until they were no longer viable and would not grow, but I see before me thousands of plants and only one barren pot.

Integrity and courage are more important values for leadership than proud displays, so Ling will be my heir."

Transcending Conformity

When we compare ourselves, our focus becomes more about conforming to other people's expectations rather than embracing what is unique in us. It seems easier at first to adapt to what others find acceptable than be different in any way. No one wants to be perceived as a failure, especially when everyone else appears to have it all together. Yet, it can be exhausting keeping up pretenses. No one can play a role indefinitely and sooner or later, illusions dissolve.

While our stories might share the same genius, no one has lived your exact circumstances with your history and essence. This means that no one else can tell your story the way only you can. We are all storytellers. We might use a different medium, yet every story deserves to be shared and witnessed. Every poem seeks a poet whose heart has been cracked open either by great pain or great joy. Lyrics court musicians, begging to be expressed. So why do we ever choose to dim our own light? Often, this is due to the earlier messages that we received. *Don't cause trouble. Don't get too big for your britches. No one will like you if you do, be or say that. Shush, don't say anything.*

It often requires effort to replace these limiting messages with more affirming ones. *Be disruptive if it means standing up for what is right. Embrace your vulnerability, but do not play insignificant. Not everyone will like you regardless, so be yourself. Let yourself be seen and heard.* You do not have to hide your imperfections for fear of ridicule or apologize for the successes in your life. As Dr. Dyer would say, "You can't feel bad enough to make anybody else's life better." Just because someone is incapable of celebrating with you does not mean you should join them in their misery. We all have shadows, namely, the rejected parts of ourselves that we have yet to fully embrace. However, we are not meant to become anyone else's shadow. Stand in your own light and own your glow.

We receive from the same Source

There is no need for comparison when we recognize that we are all receiving from the same creative source. Ideas become available to all of us. If more than one person simultaneously reaches for the same idea, we call that synchronicity. It does not make it less of an achievement. It confirms our connectedness. Just because there is no logical explanation, does not mean something cannot be so.

We do not have to begrudge anyone else's success. Copyright regulations allow for more innovation. If something has already been done one specific way, there are still other possibilities and other ways to consider. Movie themes are a prime example of this; similar storyline, different actors and directors, still worth watching. We have to be willing to look beyond our initial thinking in order to see the additional opportunities that are being made available to us. *How am I meant to add to the discovery? What further insights do I hold?*

Be an uplifter

When you express your genius in a way that encourages and uplifts others, it allows them to be more innovative as well. In 1878, Milton Wright *(November 17, 1828 ~April 3, 1917)*, a Bishop and father of Wilbur *(April 16, 1867~May 30, 1912)* and Orville Wright *(August 19, 1871 ~January 30, 1905)* brought back from his travels a model helicopter made of cork, bamboo and paper. Its blades were powered by a rubber band. Little did he know that this would be the inspiration his sons would need to build and fly the first practical airplane. Aviation, electricity and plumbing were genius ideas that were expressed and enjoyed by us. There are certainly other amazing treasures awaiting our discovery.

Whether you are a parent, stepparent, grandparent, friend, coach, aunt, uncle, neighbor or educator, if you interact with a young child or teenager in any way, you have the capacity to uplift and greatly influence their lives. Ask not what they wish to become, but rather listen for who they are in this moment. Listen to their thoughts. Hear between what is said and left unsaid. Hear the lyrics of the songs they are they listening to. Listen without criticizing but seek to understand. Be quick to praise and slower to blame and criticize. When we look for and recognize their genius, we can better assist them in realizing their full potential.

The genius in our dreams

As I began this writing, I did not expect to share about my dream experiences to the extent that I have. Along the way, I noticed how often a dream would hold a symbol or metaphor that either connected to what I would be writing about next or the writing process would call to mind a past dream. Not every dream holds significant meaning, yet studies reveal that dreaming, which occurs during deep (REM) sleep, improves problem solving, magnifies creativity and enhances memory recall, suggesting there is genius in our dreams.

Dr. Matthew Walker, a neuroscientist and professor at the University of California, Berkeley claims that "REM sleep is the only time when our brain is completely devoid of the anxiety-triggering molecule noradrenaline." This means that quality sleep can be beneficial to those of us who experience high levels of anxiety. Are you getting enough quality sleep? Are our children sleeping enough?

Dr. Walker also refers to dreaming as "overnight therapy" where REM sleep decreases our tendency to become reactive due to overwhelm. We are less reactive when we are well rested. This stage of deep sleep allows for restoration and healing and can also provide resolutions to conflicts and traumatic events of the previous day. According to Dr. Walker's research, "time spent in dream sleep is what heals."

Dreams are a great way to connect to our inner wisdom and the genius beyond our conscious mind. Many of our ancestors revered their dreams and spent time deciphering their meanings. Yet, the language of dreams is rather complex and there can be multiple interpretations. In my experience, dreams can provide information about the past, the present and possibilities for the future. I believe they provide insight into who we are, who we wish to become and how best to get to where we hope to be. Everyone who sleeps, dreams and you do not have to remember your dreams in order to experience their physical and emotional benefits.

~ PRACTICE ~

Receiving guidance from dreams

As you prepare for sleep, sit upright and breathe deeply. When you feel a sense of relaxation, set an intention for clarifying thoughts, practical solutions, new innovations that might be seeking a willing participant to come to you as you sleep. Enter this spaciousness with the intention to awaken fully rested and rejuvenated. See what thoughts you awaken with.

Before leaving your bed, take a moment to review any dreams you might have had. If there is nothing, continue this practice for a few more nights. You do not have to force anything to happen. The insight will come in due time. If not, enjoy the benefits of deeper sleep and awake feeling refreshed.

The voice within says,

I allow the genius of life to support and delight me in countless ways. I remain open to the unlimited stream of ideas that await me. I rest in the awareness that all will be revealed in Divine timing.

Chapter 10

Reverence

"Go to the sea," my grandmother would often say. She believed that the sea was the cure for just about any ailment. She sent us off without a word of caution. My cousins, my sister, my brother and I would often swim in the ocean without any adult present. *How did you know we would all remain safe?*

And I could almost hear her say, *Child, you were never unattended. I asked the sea to watch over all of you. If ever you ventured too far out, its waves would gently usher you closer to shore. And now... now I am the sea. I am the grains of sand, the starfish, the seashells. Hear my laughter in yours. See my smile in your smile. Feel my warmth in the rays of the sun, my touch in a quiet breeze. I am always near, for I am love, eternally.*

Honor our elders and tell their stories

I was raised in a culture that honored our elders and not just those who were related to us. As children on the island in Anguilla, if we were caught doing something that we should not have been doing, we could be assured that a grandparent would hear about it before we even returned home. These were not busybodies hoping to cause trouble, but elders who cared about children beyond their own. We would not dare be disrespectful to any of them or the *punishment* would be that more severe. Our grandmother's tongue-lashing was to be avoided at all costs. Still, the worst *punishment* I ever recall from her was when she made us attend three church services in one Sunday, one early morning service at the Anglican church, one at a Baptist church and then an afternoon service at a different Baptist church. Any misbehaving and she would hear about it.

I also enjoy the company of those who are wise beyond my years. Especially when they have been doing their own inner healing work, they can hold space for so much more because of all they have lived themselves. They are beyond the constant judgments and comparisons of youth. They are courageous and practical and genuinely interested in your well being. They revel in your accomplishments as though they were their own.

We must tell our stories with our elders in mind. They were not bound to any one way of living and being in this world. They went in search of work even if it meant traveling to another land. Many of them were self-taught sailors, engineers and builders or maybe they were so appreciative that their geniuses just continued to stick around. Once they honed their craft, they took on an apprentice and taught someone else. They did not limit themselves to one craft or one title. They had multiple skills. My grandmother was a seamstress, a medicine woman, a farmer, a shepherd and baked the best West Indian johnnycakes in her time.

My grandfather was a fisherman, a sailor, a marshal, a builder and if he were alive in today's world, he would also be known as a medium. He had the ability to know when people had passed on from the physical world into the spiritual realm. He would talk about it matter-of-factly. He passed on when I was just thirteen. I can still remember the first dream I had of him. It was in 1996. In my dream, he was sitting and my brother appeared as a younger version of himself asleep on our grandfather's lap. I woke from the dream feeling as though my grandfather was keeping watch over my brother. Days later, my brother shared an experience of having a gun pointed in his face by a roommate. I have no doubt that my grandfather was present at that moment and somehow affected the outcome of that experience.

Transcending Worry

May I be free of worry

May I be well

May I feel safe and at ease

May I be at peace

~ Buddhist practice

In a recent conversation with my brother, we talked about our grandmother's faith. How she prayed about everything and seemingly worried about nothing. She trusted we would be okay, and we were. There was a time my brother had been lost for a few hours. He might have been six or seven years old. We did not live on the island year-round. We only visited during the summer and he had been at a camp that was held in the center of the island. The bus inadvertently left without him and he had no idea how to get back to our grandparents' home. He did not know the name of the village where we stayed. A stranger stopped to pick him up at the side of the road, but my brother only knew our grandparents' as Mama and Papa. Because of his last name, the man figured which village he belonged and brought him to the Eastern part of the island. We never knew how many stops that man made to determine which house my brother belonged to, but sure enough, he brought him home.

Practicing Surrender

I would not say that I possess the measure of faith that my grandmother had, although there have been many opportunities to practice surrender. When I think of what it means to surrender, I recall an incident that occurred when I was about thirteen years old. I had been playing in the ocean with a group of my cousins, volleying a ball when I suddenly found myself sinking. I did not know this at the time, but the beach named Captain's Bay was known to have sudden "drop-offs." If you stepped out even just a bit, you could find yourself in deep water, which is what happened, and I did not know how to swim.

It all happened so fast. I did not struggle to stay afloat. I cannot say exactly how much time passed, but enough to recognize I was sinking and that I was waiting for someone to help me. Still, there was no sense of panic. I made no attempt to save myself. My cousin, Shawn, came to my rescue that day. When I was safely ashore is when I began to feel a sense of panic, as I started to think about all that could have happened. I remember asking myself, *why didn't I pray?*

Why didn't I pray? Why didn't I panic? Why didn't I fight to stay afloat? I guess something else within me took over and I trusted that I would be okay.

Practicing surrender is about trusting in every experience, even the ones that leave us breathless and in a constant state of uncertainty. There is always something to be gleaned when we remember that we have everything we need within us. We came into this world with nothing, yet everything. The only thing we can successfully manipulate at the hour of our birth is our breath so that our cries could be heard. Every other need is met by someone else until we become conscious and more aware of the gift of this life. *When did we stop recognizing all of life as a gift?*

When I first read this poem by Alice Walker, best known for *The Color Purple*, I was taken by her reference to the ocean as a womb. I consider the womb to be a safe place, whereas an ocean is unpredictable. I still find myself guarded around bodies of water and yet I have an affinity to water. This tendency toward fear may have been triggered by that one childhood incident even though I have taken swim classes as an adult and have worked on releasing this phobia. My mom is also not fond of the water because of an adverse childhood experience. Still, we come from a family of incredible swimmers and expert divers.

My current home is surrounded by a huge pond that connects to a lake. There was a time when I would have been too fearful to choose this house as our home. Now, I cannot imagine having a permanent

> "...We have a beautiful mother
>
> Her oceans are wombs
>
> Her wombs are oceans
>
> ~Alice Walker,
>
> *Her Blue Body Everything We Know*

residence elsewhere. While I most appreciate when my feet are firmly planted on the ground, I love the sight of water. I gladly enjoy it from a distance. I respect the water and whenever I am surrounded by it, I ask that it respects me. Swim lessons for our daughter was a top priority and I am grateful she is a strong swimmer and embraces the ocean, rivers and lakes.

I am reminded of a 2018 film titled, *'Black Kids Can't Swim,"* that chronicled the journey of a black man learning to swim as an adult. While this production highlights the cultural and financial reasons surrounding racial disparities when it comes to swimming, my greatest takeaway was Ed Accura's response to the question, *what was your biggest hurdle in learning how to swim*? "Trusting the water," he replied. "It took me close to six lessons to trust the water to support me... I figured that if huge ships can be supported by water without sinking, so could I."

Grace

Adopting a practice

I have come to define spiritual practice as the process of coming to know ourselves beyond our physical expression and visible limitations. There is no single way to initiate this ongoing process. It is more about finding something that feels good and comfortable, which allows you to embrace all aspects of who you are. Allowing yourself to feel gratitude is a spiritual practice. Painting, writing, time in nature—these are all spiritual practices. If sitting in mediation does not appeal to you, then consider adopting a moving meditation practice like Qigong or walking in silence.

We have so much available to us and yet we are not taught how to access our inner world. Imagine if we all learned this tool as children, in the comfort of our own homes? Imagine if we recognized sooner than later that our greatest challenges were opportunities to know ourselves more deeply. *What if we were taught to summon our genius and our guardian angels? What if we all knew that the wisdom of our ancestors is still available to us?*

We are the voice and hands of our ancestors

We often hear that we are the hopes and dreams of our grandparents. This is true. Much of what our grandparents endured allowed us to be as we are. Those who were held captive envisioned a time when their descendents would be free. Those who were born into poverty worked incessantly to ensure that their descendents would not want for anything. And now here we are. We are now their voices and their hands.

Insight: Embracing Life, Discovering Beauty, Grace and True Purpose

In what ways are you being called to grow beyond your history? How can you serve our ancestors' continuing legacy?

Grace

~ PRACTICE ~

Transcribing a Letter from an Ancestor

- Be prepared to write after some time in silence.
- Sit comfortably, spine upright, feet firmly planted on the ground.
- Soften your gaze and breathe deeply.
- Imagine being visited by one or more of your healed ancestors. *Who might this person or persons be? What message do they hold for you?*
- Set a timer for at least 10 minutes and write non-stop. Write whatever comes to mind, no editing. I prefer pen and paper, but use whatever medium is most comfortable for you.

The voice within says,

I am a descendent of great hopes and dreams. I aspire to be an ancestor of even greater hopes and dreams. I embrace all the adventures that lie before me with integrity, intention and purpose.

Chapter 11

Alignment

When she was just a preschooler, my daughter helped me to see that things do not always add up the way we expect. I was quizzing her on simple addition one day. I started with "two plus two" and "three plus three," and then asked, "What about one and one?" She brought her index fingers together and said, "Eleven." With all the affirming words that begin with the letter 'A,' it still amazes me that the eleventh chapter of this book is about alignment. In ancient Greece, the Pythagoreans believed in "numerical harmony," that numbers were the basis for the entire universe.

On January 27, 2020, I made a purchase at a local store totaling 111.53. Of course, the 111 caught my attention. That purchase included a journal that exclaimed write! write! write! Later that day, I became aware of an opportunity to submit an essay to a Hay House Diverse Wisdom Initiative Contest. The prize would include six months of coaching with an established Hay House author plus a chance to submit a book proposal to Hay House, one of the largest publishers of inspirational, self-help and spiritual books. On February 2nd, I sent my essay as well as a copy of the outline for this book. Then on February 18, I ordered some homeopathic remedies online from *Vitacost*, which I rarely do. The total cost of my order, 111.53. One week later, I learned that I was one of twelve aspiring authors chosen to participate in the Diverse Wisdom contest. And then March 22nd, my purchase at a pet store for my beloved Summer totaled, you guessed it, 111.53. So of course, I shared with a friend who had recently been to a medium who mentioned someone by the name of Kyle Gray, author of *Angel Numbers: The Message and Meaning Behind 11:11 and Other Number Sequences*. On page 55, this is what he writes about 111:

> You are one with all that is. Know that all you are doing and giving is for the world and all the beings in it.

And on page 40 regarding 53:

> The universe is never working against you, it's always working for you. Trust in God's plan as it unfolds.

The hand of grace...

As Dr. Dyer would say, "Divine synchronicity is always working, moving the pieces around." It is ultimately up to each one of us to notice the pieces and define how best to fit them together into our own lives. My yellow Lab named Summer left me a message last year to remind me that I was slipping into busyness. I had left a book, *Simple Wisdom for Challenging Times*, written by my friend Gail Van Kleeck, on the countertop along with an Oprah Magazine. I returned home to pages of the book and magazine, shredded and scattered all over the kitchen floor.

After a few long breaths, what caught my attention were the first and last pages that Summer left intact. The top page was about *busyness*. My eyes were drawn to these words, "when we schedule life too tightly, we leave no room for the magic." The back page still attached was about *writing*. As I read Gail's message, "one of the most important ways to nurture and heal our spirit is to write," I felt a deep resonance. Yet, other than my daily morning ritual, I was not carving out as much time to write as I would have liked.

It seems so easy at times to lose sight of what is most important. We tend to put aside what matters most in order to fulfill other obligations. While I have a long list of books to read and re-read during retirement, I have decided to no longer put aside my writing. I am grateful for the gentler reminders that come in the form of torn pages from a book that could easily be replaced. Within weeks of Summer's message, I began carving out more time to write. Months later (September 28, 2019), I shared about this experience in a blog post with photos if you are curious about the message that came in the form of a mess.

Following the guidance

In November 2019, I dreamt of receiving a book from an unknown male figure. Within weeks of this dream, I had a sense of what each chapter of this book would be about, beginning with the words *healing and transcending* as seen in the outline. I did consider replacing some of the original words that appeared to me in October 2015. Like Chapter 17 on *Courage*, initially I had no idea where to begin with the chapters on *Enduring, Creation* and *Emergence*. I did end up changing the H- in Hope from Honor to Harmony. Although I wanted to honor the original outline, the word *Harmony* resonates deeply with my love of music and dance. And our current state of our world confirms my intuition about the importance of this message.

> Dream journal: November 2, 2019...*He is standing to my left wearing a crimson robe. He steps forward and offers me a book. "I give you giok," he says. I accept this book. The only detail I notice is its color, red.*

When I opened my eyes that morning, I was most curious about the fact that this man spoke a word that was unfamiliar to me, yet I knew its spelling. Though I could see the book I was given, I was unable to recall what was written on its cover. I did an internet search of the word 'giok' and discovered it to be an Indonesian word, meaning *Jade*. Jade is a gemstone, commonly seen in shades of green, symbolizing purity. It is also the name I had chosen for our second-born daughter. Can you venture to guess what the *expression number* for the name Jade is? It is number eleven.

The early Greeks, Hebrews and the Chaldeans, an ancient tribe of Mesopotamia practiced *arithmomancy*, also known as "number divination," where words become numbers when their values are added together. These numbers are then said to have an expression that orients a person towards certain abilities and traits. My expression number is *number one* whether I use my full maiden name or my full married name. While I would not describe myself as "extremely ambitious or fearless," as expressed by *number ones*, I do resonate with the quality of perseverance and the need for freedom to make my own decisions. If you are interested, there are multiple websites that provide an expression number calculator.

Transcending Displacement

I once heard Ta-Nehisi Coates, author of *Between the World and Me*, say that he is not someone charged with inspiring hope. I appreciated his descriptive imagery, hearing about his grandmother, his pride in blackness, and other insights into how some black men view the world. I could relate to his reverence for libraries and writing, his intense quest for understanding and a thirst for true freedom. This book also prompted me to think about how often our life experiences cause us to become displaced from our truest essence—love, hope and a sense of aliveness.

I recall feeling a sense of displacement when life did not align with my expectations of how it should be. My version of the American dream was to have two children, preferably daughters, about two years apart who would become best friends and always be there for each other. Growing up, not only did I have siblings, but I also had numerous cousins who felt more like stepsisters and brothers. We had such fun together. How could I raise an only child, especially knowing she would not have nearby cousins to befriend? I wanted to give our daughter the best of my childhood experiences. Yet, she has given me greater insight into what it means to connect and build meaningful relationships beyond blood relation. I have revised my definition of what it means to be family.

Allow space for the unexpected

We also experience feelings of displacement when our self-worth is tied to just one idea of how we must exist in this world. According to a January 2020 study by the Centers for Disease Control and Prevention, farmers are currently among the highest occupation to die by suicide because of debt and an uncertain future. In recent times, we have become even more aware of the fact that life can drastically rearrange our plans and summon us to depths we had no idea existed. Business ventures could fail, relationships might not be ever after, well-crafted plans may not come together as anticipated. This is life. We cannot burn down the entire orchard because several trees did not bear fruit. The storms of our lives must not cause us to lose hope.

Our ancestors held on to hope, which allowed us to exist as we do today. And now it is up to us to give life a fair chance to redeem itself. New business ventures could be awaiting us. When it comes to love, we can start anew, sometimes with the same partner but build a mutually enriching relationship this time around. We can decide not to judge our spouse by every disappointment of the past but embrace their willingness to become a better expression of their former self. This reminds me of a humorous anniversary card I once bought, "I love you exactly as you are, but don't get any worse." If what is broken cannot be repaired, then treasure the joys once shared as you determine the best way to say goodbye. Write a new script for the future you wish to participate in. That inner restlessness you might be feeling is often a call to trust more, not give up. When we choose life no matter how difficult that choice becomes, we often get to witness extraordinary possibilities. When we choose innovation over frustration and a sense of adventure over steadfast control of one outcome, we begin to see how mystical life truly is.

Aligning with integrity

In psychological terms, displacement also refers to the tendency to direct frustration or blame unto a person simply because they are "safer" or more accessible than the actual target of our intense emotions. We might unfairly chastise a child or lash out at a spouse because of an issue at work, a life circumstance or something beyond anyone's control. A bad week is not an excuse to wield insults at someone who has been a long-time friend. Yet as social media demonstrates, many of us seem to continuously displace our emotions of frustration and anger. *Freedom of Speech* should not be interpreted as freedom to be cruel to another human being. Abusive language is abuse. Similarly, people in power displace their undealt-with emotions as well. How did we get so far out of alignment with who we really are?

I was about the age of twelve when I first realized what it meant to lose integrity. My mom sent me to the neighborhood store to purchase a loaf of bread for the next day. My six-year-old brother wanted to come along. While at the store, I noticed a glazed loaf of cinnamon bread that looked more appealing than the sliced white bread I was told to buy. I decided I would take just a small piece. I offered a piece to my brother as well. And then I turned and made eye contact with the storeowner. We were caught. He motioned to have me bring the bread I was attempting to place back onto the shelf. This is the bread I had to take home to my mother. As soon as I entered the door, I showed her the bread and explained how my brother had only taken a small piece and the storeowner caught him. She was quite upset. I remember how badly my stomach hurt that night, not because I was caught, but because I chose to lie about it and my brother was chastised for something he didn't do—something I was too afraid to own up to.

Integrity is that inner flutter we feel when our words are not in alignment with truth and honor. I have felt it as a hollowing sensation in the area right below the diaphragm when I have said something with an edge of sarcasm that digs a little deeper than intended or when I choose at first to ignore a meme shared on social media that was hurtful, unintentionally so, but still hurtful. There are times when silence is absolutely the best response. *Just ignore it*, my conscious mind would say. We do not have to attend every argument we are invited to. But when something deep inside me suffers a bit longer, I recognize this as a call to respond, authentically and with compassion. In recent times, I have gained a greater understanding of Dr. King's admonition that silence can be a form of betrayal to oneself. When someone you care about hurts you, it must be addressed. If not, resentment spawns an even greater hurt.

We can all learn from each other. Our views vary because of our experiences, our background and differing thoughts. If you have never lived in a body that has experienced chronic pain, you may not be able to understand someone else's need to take every precaution possible with a novel virus. Even if you have experienced an anxious thought, you may not understand fully the effects of constant stress and anxiety on the body. Likewise, you cannot expect someone to fully understand your plight because they have lived a totally different experience. It is important that we each express our sense of truth not necessarily to change someone else's viewpoint but to say, *this is how I have experienced this reality*. And we can do so with compassion. When did it become okay to demean another person because of their differing views? *Be impeccable with your word* writes Toltec wisdom author Don Miguel Ruiz. "Use the power of your word in the direction of truth and love."

It seems imperative that we align with integrity in order to remedy the divisiveness that continues to plague our society. If we continually displace our unhealed emotions onto family, friends or even strangers, we risk causing further harm. We need to stop, says young peacemaker, Mattie Stepanek *(July 17, 1990 ~ June 22, 2004)* in his poem, *"For Our World."*

> *"We need to stop.*
> *Just stop.*
> *Stop for a moment...*
> *Before anybody*
> *Says or does anything*
> *That may hurt anyone else.*
>
> *We need to be silent.*
> *Just silent.*
> *Silent for a moment...*
>
> *Before we forever lose*
> *The blessing of songs*
>
> *That grow in our hearts..."*

It is also important that we realize that broken systems can be an opportunity for us to be a part of rebuilding and repair. Protests serve to bring awareness. Now that we are aware, what do we do next? Do we continue to place the responsibility of change solely on governing officials and school systems? Or, can we go into the schools and neighboring communities individually or in groups and inquire, how might I serve? Well, when it is safe to do so once again. Imagine if the millions who attend marches decide to become a *Big Brother* or *Big Sister* to a lonely child? How can we still connect and still be involved during these times?

What has your life aligned you with? What is your current definition of family? How are you being called to serve?

~ PRACTICE ~

Adopting a Personal Code of Honor

A personal code of honor can serve to keep us in integrity with our highest values. You might want to revisit The Sacred Tree Practice in Chapter 4 to reassess what you hold to be sacred.

Here are three statements from my own personal statement:

1. I will do all that I can to honor this vessel that houses my inner being.
2. I will remain open to learning and growing and deepening my understanding of myself, others and the world around me.
3. I will embrace opportunities to uplift, encourage, inspire and empower my fellow human beings.

The voice within says,

I seek to be in integrity with the highest expression of all that I am. As I honor all aspects of myself, I honor the Source of my creation. I use the power of my words to uplift, encourage, inspire and empower. I act in accordance with my deepest wisdom.

Insight: Embracing Life, Discovering Beauty, Grace and True Purpose

Chapter 12

Creation

Dream Journal: May 17, 2017…… *Last night I dreamt of a young child who appeared to be alone on a beach. Though blind, she could see the sun's shadow. Evening after evening, she existed alone, knowing when the sun appeared by its shadow. She would then sit, lie down or stand and just stare and stare at the sun's shadow until one day she began to see a little speck of light. The more she stared, the larger and brighter this little light became.*

In her excitement, she concentrated even more, focusing and focusing until she could no longer look at the sun. It was then that she was able to see fully. The sun's light had given her vision.

She looked around and saw barren land and water. And with such joy in her heart combined with the sun's light, her mind began to think in images and in color.

Anything she could think of became manifest.

Up until that point, her only nourishment came through the soles of her bare feet, absorbing minerals and fluids from the Earth.

Harnessing the energy of the sun, she continued to create. She created trees and flowers, fruit and animals and everything else around her.

She began to play even more with her abilities until she created a playmate in her image.

And since she had the ability to create, everything she created also had the ability to create.

The playmates could not see their own faces, only each other. The more of them that began to exist, the more creative they became in choosing different shapes and colors.

Grace

I woke up with the thought that God created Mother Earth and Father Sun, who then bore a single human child. This one child became the creator of every other child that became she, he, him, her or they. And now here we are, her descendents, just making the rest up as we go along, trying to find our favorite playmate, comparing ourselves, fighting with each other about which of us is better, maturing in body, yet often resorting to our childish ways. This would explain so much.

When I consider the power of imagination, it causes me to be discerning about the visions shared by all visionaries. Some messages resonate and some do not. I am grateful I do not hear the voice of God outside of myself telling me exactly what I must do. How do we distinguish the Divine from our own mental constructs? How do we know which visions to trust when they have not been our own? A male friend once said, *the only thing we can know for sure is that we exist.* My response to that is, *how would we know we exist if we did not have others to relate to?*

"Everything that exists was once imagined," says Wayne Dyer. Again, I am grateful that not everything I imagine becomes a reality. I can still recall the first horror movie I watched when I was about twelve or thirteen. It was about a rabid St. Bernard dog. I became so frightened of dogs in general, I imagined them all to be dangerous. I have become extremely selective about which television shows and movies I watch, so I cannot fully explain the vivid images that arise in my mind. In writing this book, I now realize I do not have to. I choose to share my experience; you get to choose what resonates and what does not. I have learned to watch with curiosity and observe without judgment or expectation as words or images appear behind my closed eyes. I hear of people who see images, colors and other people's auras. I do not have these abilities. I feel energies, though. I believe that on some level we all do. We feel sensations in our body that we cannot explain fully, so many of us become anxious, wondering, *what is wrong with me?* We are not taught how to explore these sensations. Instead, we either choose to ignore them, numb ourselves to them or allow them to control us.

> *"You must give birth to your images. They are the future waiting to be born... fear not the strangeness you feel. The future must enter into you long before it happens....Just wait for the birth...for the hour of new clarity.* ~ Rainer Maria Rilke (December 4, 1975 ~December 29, 1926) in *Letters to a Young Poet*, letter #3

Transcending "Original Sin"

Back in November 2019 when I wrote the phrase *healing and transcending* "original sin," I had no idea of how this chapter might evolve. Even as a child I was confused by the idea of being born a sinner. I remember thinking, *I do not like being blamed for something I did not do*. This morning (June 29, 2020) I awoke from a dream where someone unknown to me used a vehicle to intentionally cause damage to property that was not his own. The driver had clearly been angry about something and decided to cause destruction. This awakened me to the realization that destruction is the direct opposite of creation. Hatred and misuse of power in all its forms, physical, emotional, sexual, verbal—these are some of the most destructive forces that threaten our existence.

These are the forces that lead to continued suffering and oppression.

We can create or we can destroy

We are incredibly powerful beings. The stories we tell can enliven or destroy. With just our words we can illuminate a person, or we can demean them. We can spark healing, or we can cause great hurt. We can be honoring, or we can be deceptive. Our thoughts and our words guide our behaviors, our actions and our interactions. They influence how we relate to one another and the world around us. The cost of billboards and advertisements confirm the power of words to inspire, to empower and in some cases, to mislead and manipulate our emotions.

Anything that divides seeks to destroy. Anything that unites supports creation. These words arise from within me when I consider the concept of creation. To create is to gather substances and bring something even more extraordinary into existence. It is to materialize an idea or express a feeling that someone else can connect to. Creativity brings people together. We connect through artistic endeavors, music, theater, dance, poetry. On the other hand, anything that divides, namely, hatred, injustice, condemnation lead to destruction. In *Jesus and the Disinherited* by Howard Thurman, originally published in 1949, he describes "fear, hypocrisy and hatred" as the "three hounds of hell."

Even religious beliefs can be a source of unity or division. *If an idea or belief leads to the destruction of an innocent life, how can that be supported by the Source of all creation?* I appreciate the statement made by Arturo Paoli (*November 30, 1912 ~ July 13, 2015*) an Italian priest who believed that "to be religious is to give your life so that the world may be more beautiful, more just, more at peace; it is to prevent egotistical and self-serving ends from disrupting the harmony of the whole." Creation restores wholeness.

Be vulnerable and creative

In his book, *"Original Blessing"* Episcopal priest Matthew Fox writes,

> *"Vulnerability is no excuse for not creating, just as fear is no excuse for lack of courage and despair is no excuse for the lack of hope…vulnerability produces creativity, which requires a capacity to get hurt. Our images can hurt us, but only temporarily. To kill or forget or neglect our images is far more lethal…"*

Our most vulnerable moments can be our most creative ones. Poetry and songs illustrate the depths that love and loss can take us to. How many books would go unwritten if we were not vulnerable beings with the desire to find meaning, connect and share with others? We cannot always know our greatest strengths until we have faced our most painful moments. We often create from a place of necessity, building anew when what previously existed cannot be easily restored. We also cannot know how sharing about our darkest times can light the way for someone else.

We can often conjure up enough reasons not to do something that is worthwhile. There will always be some distraction that beckons our attention. Yet, our soul longs to express what we hold in our hearts and in our imaginations. To ignore this longing can lead to regret. "Regret for the things we did can be tempered by time; it is regret for the things we did not do that is inconsolable," said American journalist Sydney J. Harris (*September 14, 1917 ~ December 7, 1986*).

Feelings of vulnerability might be necessary to curb our egocentric tendencies, allowing us to consider our true motives. What is one's intention in sharing openly about their life experiences? *Is sharing my personal story to inspire others worth the risk of my privacy?* When viewed this way, feelings of vulnerability serve a purpose, rather than as an excuse.

Rebuild and Restore

My Caribbean family have experienced way too many hurricanes in one lifetime that have left heaps of destruction. It takes many months to restore electricity, phone service, schools and jobs. Time after time, we have had to rebuild, starting over with just an ounce of hope, yet always helping one another. With tourism being the sole industry, taking years to fully recover, it seems that rebuilding and recovery has been a constant state.

The Greek philosopher Heraclitus *(c. 540 B.C.E. ~ c. 480)* saw destruction as just another aspect of change, allowing for the birth of something new. While commonly seen as a destructive element, Heraclitus saw fire as the greatest symbol of creation, stating that the world would cease to exist without it. Fire forms and it transforms. It forms earth and it transforms metal to liquid. As one thing perishes, something else emerges. Likewise, the *fires* that threaten to destroy us also prepare us for the emergence of something new. *How will I be transformed by the fires in my life?* How will you?

There are times when life carves out new roads for us to follow. We must then look to replace unrealized dreams with new ones. The beauty of this life is that we can make detours and still find ourselves unto a more authentic path, exactly where we hoped to end up. We can embrace the visible and the mystical in the same breath. Each day is another opportunity to create something. *What is your hope for this day? What is your inner longing?* Call upon your genius who might have a few creative ideas waiting to be expressed by you. Observe your days and follow the guidance that comes in various forms. Pay attention to your nightly dreams as well.

~ PRACTICE ~

Clarifying Your Hopes and Dreams

Take two minutes of your morning to set an intention for the day. What is one thing you hope for in this day? It does not have to be an accomplishment. It could be as simple as *I hope to experience one unexpected joy today* or *May I be a light of hope for someone.* Your hope might be to receive further insight into a specific problem. Set the intention and remain open to unexpected ways the guidance might come.

Whenever possible, set aside more time to first do the *Harmonizing the Heart, Mind and Body Practice* from Chapter 5. Then, consider spending another ten to fifteen minutes writing, drawing or painting your hopes and dreams for this month, this year and so forth.

What do you wish to have more of in your life? Calm? Fun? Connection? Solitude? This can be done at anytime of the year. I do this annually on my birthday.

May your hopes and dreams be realized in the best way possible that serves the highest good of all beings.

The voice within says,

I welcome my creative gifts that serve to infuse a sense of aliveness, delight and wonder into my life. I greet the arrival of each morning with gratitude and hopeful awareness. I bless those I encounter throughout my day and I receive inspiration as I give generously.

Chapter 13

Enduring

"Nothing endures but change," said Heraclitus. He was known as the 'dark' philosopher because his writings were not easily understood. His belief that "all things are one and the same," was often the subject of ridicule. "Living and dead, waking and sleeping, young and old," he saw these not as opposites but as the same thing. As Heraclitus would say, we arise into life, vanish into death, everything changes, yet remains the same. Albert Einstein (*March 14, 1879 ~ April 18, 1955*) might agree since "energy cannot be created or destroyed," only transformed. Similarly, although our physical form changes, the essence of who we are remains the same.

Dreams of my grandmother

I still remember the first time I dreamt of my grandmother. I stood alone in the office where my husband and I started our practice, in a space that was doable, but not ideal, on the second floor of a building with no elevator. My grandmother appeared to me as though she wanted to say something. Years before when I dreamt of my grandfather, I just observed him, but he said nothing. For some reason, even in my dream state, the thought of the dead being able to speak frightened me. I did what I could to avoid hearing what my grandmother had to tell me. Suddenly I found myself in what appeared to be a much larger office. This was before I recorded my dreams, so the images are not as clear as I now write about this. I do remember that there were many plants all around this office, lots of greenery.

Sometime after, my husband and I were approached by our landlord. The thrift store on the first floor of our office building was relocating and that larger space would be available to us. It was not until after we were completely moved in (March 2003) that I recalled my dream. I was alone in our new space one evening, arranging ficus trees and other plants that everyone had gifted us. It then occurred to me that this space was similar to what my grandmother had shown me despite my unwillingness to listen. Now seventeen years later, our current office feels even more like the space I envisioned years ago.

Another dream of my grandmother came years later when I was eleven weeks pregnant.

> Journal entry: November 23, 2007...*I had a dream last night that Mama was sitting on my bed holding a baby girl. It scared me a little. I asked, "What are you doing here?" "But you're dead," I told her, and she disappeared. I am hoping that this dream holds no meaning. I love you already baby. I want

so much for you to enter this world and be a part of our family. It doesn't matter if you are a boy or a girl...just that you are.

A few days after this dream encounter, I was evaluated for a cerclage, a medical procedure where the cervix is sutured to prevent premature dilation. There were no signs of an incompetent cervix and so this procedure was not recommended. Still, about two weeks later, I lost this pregnancy. Chromosomal studies later revealed that it had been a baby girl. Although we never officially named her, I refer to her as "Baby Hope." I recall how hopeful I had been at least for the first eleven weeks. I now take comfort in knowing that she is with my grandmother and my other babies who fly with the angels. I believe that everyone we have loved and lost are indeed everywhere. Sometimes we are visited in our dreams and other times we get glimpses in that space between sleep and wakefulness.

Love is enduring

We do not ever stop grieving the loss of love. Once created, love can never be destroyed. Love is love is love is love. The length of a life does not determine the length of grief. What is most helpful is for this to be understood; No one wants to hurt indefinitely. No well-adjusted person wants to be the cause of another person's sadness. Still, no amount of wishing for pain to just go way causes it to do so. Well, miracles do happen. But more often than not, healing is an enduring process. Gratitude helps. I am grateful for the people who have the capacity to understand this experience even though they might not have lived it themselves. Comfort helps. It is a gift of grace to receive comfort from others. Still, we have to be open to receiving it.

Grace is enduring

I was reading the comments on a recent social media post. It seems that the word 'grace' has become somewhat marred by its religious association. I wish for everyone to recognize that not every religious practice condemns the free expression of individuals who do not cause malice to another. Howard Washington Thurman wrote, "Jesus rejected hatred because he saw that hatred meant death to the mind, death to the spirit, and death to communion with his father. He affirmed life; and hatred was the great denial." The Jesus I connect to affirms life and the Christ within me says, *just like the fish, there are a multitude of ways*. Still, there will be people, living from a place of fear, who use the gospel to support hatred and the misuse of power.

My daughter recently said, *"Mom with everything that is happening, I don't know if I still believe in God."* To which I responded, *"It's okay my love, you don't have to believe in God, just know that goodness exists in this world."* What we believe matters. However, it is also my belief that we do not have to all believe the same thing. In my eyes, mutual respect and the freedom to decide for ourselves matter even more. I will continue to trust that my faith is strong enough for the both of us as she determines what resonates with her soul's wisdom. Grace is enduring and freely given, no exceptions.

Transcending Unforgiveness

You forgive too easily, a friend once said. That might be true, and

I also distance myself to avoid being hurt again. I read a post recently where someone wrote, *"just because I have not offered forgiveness to the person who harmed me, it does not mean that I am still wounded and unhealed."* We also hear that *forgiveness is something we give to ourselves*, not to the person or persons who caused us harm. Another definition, one that most resonates with me was offered by a guest of the Oprah Winfrey Show who said, "Forgiveness is the letting go of the hope that the past could have been any different." By this definition, transcending unforgiveness is more about allowing ourselves the space to grow and evolve and become a better expression of our past selves. In other words, we cannot undo the past, our mistakes or anyone else's. However, we can move forward with the wisdom gathered from every experience.

Letters of forgiveness

In Chapter 4, I shared a letter I wrote to my biological father in April 2011, two years after I learned the circumstances of my birth. Though I have never seen a photo of him, he appeared in a dream in March 2009. There was no clear image of his face, just a knowing that it was him. When I shared with my mom and one of my aunts, they made sense of the message I received. "I'm sorry, tell your mother" is the whispered phrase I awakened with. At the age of thirty-five, I learned for the time that my mom had been assaulted and I was conceived as a result.

> April 30, 2011...*A Letter to My...What of you is in me? I exist because of you. So, by definition, you are my father. I never*

> *knew you although you knew of me. I do not love you, but I do not despise you either. It makes me sad to know that I was not created out of love. How is it that I can love so deeply despite this? I was not loved by you, but I was loved. I was not created out of your love, but I was created out of God's love. My hope is that the best of you is in me. That is all. Goodnight.*

In March of 2012, I reread this letter and something interesting happened. As soon as I finished reading, I felt an overwhelming presence that I described at the time as "a sensation of being encompassed by love and all the intensity that typically bubbles up with this emotion; only it was coming from outside of me." That day, I wrote a second letter.

> *March 29, 2012…A Letter to My Father…*
> *You were not able to love me when you were physically present in this world. You may not have known how to. Where you are, I assume you are now healed. Today for the first time, I was able to feel the sensation of love when my thoughts were on you. I did not know that is what I needed. Somehow you did. So, thank you. My heart is now open to you…*

Now as I re-read these letters, the intensity of emotions I felt at those times is not the same. *What do I feel when I think of my biological father?* At this moment, there is no emotional charge. This might be due to the reality that my needs have changed. Eight years ago, I needed to experience his energetic presence. And now, I have completely released the hope that my past could have been any different. I am who I am.

Interestingly, in 2015, I reconnected with a friend I met in my first year of college who ended up sharing details about my biological father later that year. "I knew her father," his brother said when my friend mentioned we had recently spoken. Even though we shared ties to the island of Anguilla, neither of us had any idea how interconnected our lives really were. His brother went on to say that my biological father was a talented builder and he also stated, "He wasn't a bad man." I imagine some part of me appreciate knowing this as well. Still, what are the chances I would learn about my biological father from someone I met thousands of miles away from where I was born? What are the chances that I would receive this information decades later, at a time when I never imagined I would learn anything else about the man who fathered me?

Establishing clear boundaries

It is important that we establish clear boundaries not only in our relationships, but also with our history and with our emotions. According to Dr. Judith Swack in her course Healing from the Body Level Up (HBLU),

> "To have boundaries in a given context means that you remain yourself with a

> strong sense of identity despite what is going on around you. When you have boundaries with other people, you remain who you are and you connect, **but not merge**, with the *other* person. When you have boundaries with your history, it means that who you are as a person is much more that a series of experiences from your past. When you have boundaries with an emotion, it means you *feel* that emotion. It's you *having* an emotion rather than becoming swept up, carried away or disappearing into an emotion. When you have relationship boundaries, it's you having a relationship with another person rather than you disappearing in the relationship with another person."
> ~Judith A. Swack, Ph.D., HBLU Training Manual, page 96.

Establishing clear boundaries can be an important first step in transcending unforgiveness. It provides clarity, recognizing that our history does not define who we are in the present moment. It is still our choice to respond appropriately in our interactions, while maintaining a solid sense of self. It also occurs to me that unclear boundaries could explain the rise in personal *attacks* on social media. The ease of our connectedness on these platforms seems to blur certain lines. We are less inclined to carefully consider an appropriate response versus a disproportionate reaction.

When it comes to psychic connections, it is also important to have well-established boundaries. I recall a moment years ago when a friend requested that I communicate with one of her deceased relatives. I quickly responded that I was not a medium and I had no intention of doing this. In the early morning hours, I awoke with a stream of thoughts that contained words that were not a part of my vernacular. When I shared this with my friend, she was familiar with the phrases and was grateful for this message from her grandmother. I, on the other hand, was less than thrilled. I have learned to secure my psychic boundaries since then. I will share my practice at the close of this chapter.

Addressing limiting beliefs

Our limiting beliefs are what we unconsciously hold to be true. They often arise in childhood, drawn from a limited perspective of all that we have yet to experience. They can also be adopted in adulthood from a source we admire, or as a result of a traumatic event. These beliefs impact our ability to view the world objectively. Instead, in our day to day lives, we continue to seek validation of that belief. We consciously or unconsciously deny or dismiss anything that opposes what we have come to believe. We develop phobias without understanding the origins of these paralyzing beliefs.

The problem is that whatever we believe, continues to be true even though our lens might be skewed. For example, the belief that *I am unlovable.* If someone believes that they are unworthy of love, they will stay in a relationship that is dishonoring, never realizing that they can have their needs met in a healthy manner. If someone believes the world is bleak and hostile, they will find validation of this belief. I am not suggesting that we deny our real-life problems; I am suggesting that we maintain a balanced view. There is bad and there is good. In fact, there is plenty of good if we allow ourselves to see it. In some ways, I even understand Shakespeare's proclamation, "for there is nothing either good or bad but thinking makes it so." It is often what we interpret as *bad* that uncovers something good.

Cry, scream, stomp...

No one is immune to life challenges that bring us to our depths and strain our inner resolve. We have to be kind to ourselves, but especially when life is upended. Being kind does not equate with being perfectly composed in every moment. Give yourself permission to cry, to scream, to stomp, anything other than inflict harm or cause irreversible damage. Forgive yourself. Forgive your initial thoughts and reactions. Forgive what you did not know, what you could not understand. Forgive your past, your unrealized hopes and dreams.

Allow yourself to grieve. Grief is not destructive. It is healing and restorative to the body, to the mind and to the soul. On the other hand, unexpressed grief is like a dam where water spills over the top from time to time. Then one day without warning, the impounded waters release with such force that can be destructive. You were not created to cause destruction. You were created to affirm life.

~ PRACTICE ~

Establishing a healthy boundary

As always, take a few minutes to get centered and connect with your breath. If you are inclined, consider inviting Archangel Michael into your space. Saint Michael the Archangel is said to provide divine protection with his luminous blue light. He carries with him a sword to cut the chains of unwanted attachments. Imagine yourself surrounded by this sacred blue light. Imagine him cutting the chords or chains that bind you in any unwanted way.

See yourself with someone whom you wish to establish a healthy boundary. Allow yourself to feel a sense of connection to this person, while maintaining a strong sense of self. Repeat this practice as many times as needed and with every person you wish to secure a firm boundary. Bring this awareness into all of your interactions.

In terms of psychic boundaries, I do this practice before bed with the image of Archangel Michael being present. I set the intention only to have spiritual connections that serve my well-being and my highest purpose.

The voice within says,

I am a force for good and I rejoice in the goodness that exists in all. I extend forgiveness and receive forgiveness from a place of solidity within. I embrace my humanness and my mystical nature. I accept the hand of grace.

Chapter 14

Presence

July 2, 2020…How fitting it is that I am in Gail's presence as I begin this chapter. Here we are, sitting out on her patio, still observing the physical distancing recommendations due to the pandemic. It has been some time since we last shared a writing space. Charlie, her Australian Labradoodle decides to take a seat atop one of the patio chairs. So, it is the three of us on this balmy Thursday just after noontime. My chair is positioned comfortably under a tree next to Gail's garden. She shares about the flowers she recently planted.

"I haven't planted much of anything this year," I started to say.

"But you have," Gail offers. "You have been gardening your inner landscape with your writing."

"Yes, indeed I have."

When we are in the presence of someone who is warm and affirming, it is easy to recognize the best in ourselves. Even in our silence at a distance, there is a sense of being embraced and fully supported.

Being an affirming presence

So much of our life is spent comparing ourselves to one another and trying to determine where we fit into this amazing blueprint. We often desire to emulate someone else's impressive traits rather than embrace qualities that allow us to evolve into the best version of ourselves. However, we can never change ourselves enough to become anything other than who we are. It is our differences and unique attributes that allow for meaningful connections and enriching experiences. "Our similarities bring us to a common ground; our differences allow us to be fascinated by each other," writes American novelist Tom Robbins.

When we take a moment to be fully present to someone and become fascinated by them, something extraordinary happens. We hear them, not just with our ears but through our hearts. We see them, not just with our eyes, but through our innermost being. In doing so, we embolden them to see the beauty of themselves. Through this exchange, we also give ourselves permission to exist as we are with everything that adds character to our incredible design.

I recall a moment years ago when I showed up a bit early for an appointment with my dentist only to find that I was one week and fifteen minutes early. I decided to use this unscheduled time to visit my hairdresser who takes clients on a first-come-first-serve basis rather than by appointment. I figured I could just show up an hour before she opened, sit in the lobby of the building and prepare an article while I waited. Soon after, another woman joined me in the wait. We greeted each other and her curiosity about my stack of books sparked a heartfelt conversation.

She tearfully shared that she had been married for 33 years but now considering a divorce. She was scheduled to meet with an attorney later that day. She realized that she needed to say this out loud to at least one person who would not judge her or her husband. The more we spoke, the more it became clear that she needed to give this more consideration. We spoke for well over an hour and as it turns out, the salon remained closed. So, I did not have my teeth cleaned or my hair trimmed that day, but I received a hug from a stranger and my heart was filled.

People are placed upon your path

Seventeen years ago (2003), I was gifted a book by a gentleman, someone who had been a patient in my practice. I graciously accepted this gift even though it felt odd at the time. He had been a man of few words and our interaction never extended beyond his physical care, so I was surprised by this gift. Some time after his final visit, I read his obituary in our local newspaper and I immediately thought of this book. Each time I would re-arrange my bookshelf and considered donating it, I would end up retrieving it and place it back on the shelf where it continued to sit.

I made multiple attempts to read this spiritual title about the life of Paramahansa Yogananda, *Autobiography of a Yogi*, but it was not until November 2013, about 10 years after receiving it, that I was able to read this text and absorb it fully. This was a clear reminder that people are placed upon our paths and provide extraordinary gifts that we may not yet be aware of. I believe that we grow into the people we become in part because of the people we meet along the way.

Transcending Regret

In her book, *The Top Five Regrets of the Dying*, Australian author and songwriter Bronnie Ware shares that the most common regret of those facing death was leaving this world with unfulfilled dreams. People who were terminally ill reportedly wished that they had lived more courageously and chosen the life they truly wanted rather than the one that had been expected of them. For us who are still here, it is never too late to consider the longings of our heart. *How can you begin to live more authentically in this moment? What ardent dream still calls to you? What one step can you take today in the direction of that dream?*

Honor your dreams

At times it seems as though we are following a societal outline that requires us to "learn whatever is taught, protect what you have, create financial security so that you can one day retire and spend your days doing whatever you want." We do hear *follow your dreams*, but often with a stipulation that those dreams be practical. We owe it ourselves to create the life we imagine even if the present terrain does not seem conducive to creating that life. Acknowledge where you are and consider what is necessary to not only survive, but to thrive. "The entire universe is inside you," said Rumi. With this in mind, you can be assured that help and guidance will show up in unexpected ways. You are deserving of a life of prosperity and joy. Honor your dreams and as Dr. Dyer would say, "Don't die with your music still in you."

Nurture your relationships

When we consider our regrets, most of us would agree that time spent with the people in our lives matter more than everyday responsibilities and tasks. Even someone like me who values solitude recognizes the value of the people in my life. While my maternal grandparents were entrusted with my care, there were also aunts and uncles still at home who looked after me as well. Along the way, they have been others who have mothered or fathered me in some way. For each of these persons, I am eternally grateful.

Still, obligations and busyness tend to easily steal our time and create unwanted distance between us and those we care most about. Relationships, from our most casual to our most intimate, require nurturing if they are to continue to exist, evolve and be mutually beneficial. Even a five-minute phone call to say *I love you* and *you matter to me* makes a difference. I used to think differently, that if I didn't have twenty minutes to spare, I would prefer to wait until I did. Weeks would turn into months and I would find myself consumed with regret for not being in touch with those who mean the world to me.

However, it is never late to begin again if that person is only a phone call or postcard away. It might seem a bit awkward at first, but one phone call can turn into five and the bond is reestablished. Being present to the people in our lives is one of the greatest gifts we can give and simultaneously receive. We can still cherish our moments of solitude, recognizing that our relationship to ourselves is also of utmost value.

Exercise Your Senses

Embrace the present moment we often hear and yet our minds are more inclined to wander back to a past event, ahead to a future time or find some other means of distraction. How do we remain fully present to this moment? I have realized the importance of training my five senses. At least once a day I take a few minutes to check in with my body. What do I notice within and around me? What do I hear, smell, taste? If I am outside, I might pick up a rock or a stick. How does this feel in my hands?

There is always something new and interesting in our current environment. It is up to us to pause and take notice. Give yourself permission to take this valuable time each day to exercise your senses; notice, listen, smell, taste and touch.

~ PRACTICE ~

Restoring a bond of being

- In a comfortable position, take a few deep, cleansing breaths.
- Bring your awareness to your heart.
- Call to mind someone with whom you feel a connection but have lost touch with. This person can be anywhere in the world. It might also be someone in your home.
- Imagine a current of energy flowing between the two of you. Feel this bond strengthening with each breath.
- When you are ready, decide on which action to take. Will you send a digital message, a card, a handwritten note, make a phone call, or initiate a conversation if this person is nearby?

The voice within says,

I create the time and space in my life to nurture my dreams and my relationships. I am present to others I meet along the path, assisting them in ways that are most honoring of my gifts and remaining open to the guidance that they hold for me. I delight in finding new ways to fulfill my soul's dreams.

Insight: Embracing Life, Discovering Beauty, Grace and True Purpose

Chapter 15

Ease

It is not our natural state to struggle. We are not meant to live each day in a constant battle with ourselves or with each other, fighting for the right to exist as we are, for our body autonomy, our health or the well being of our loved ones. We were created for wellness, to thrive, to create, to live in harmony with each other and in harmony with the lands that we occupy. This does not mean that we should never experience challenges or obstacles. It means that we can find our way around obstacles with greater ease, finding alternate routes when necessary, becoming more resourceful as needed. So, when did we accept that life would be a constant struggle?

Our country's most recent upheaval has called to mind all that my ancestors endured for me to exist as I am today. I imagine that their greatest struggle was not with the land or the elements. They communed with nature and found ways to cultivate the land and secure food. They were innovative and created tools and weapons to protect against the wild. So, I imagine their struggle was with each other when the value of power and material wealth superseded the value of life and individual freedom. I imagine that is when their tendency to struggle began and possibly when ours did too.

We are all meant to be free

Baroness Karen Blixen also known under her pen names Isak Dinesen and Tania Blixen *(April 17, 1885 ~ September 7, 1962)* wrote, 'If only I could live and serve the world that after me there should never again be birds in cages." If you were created to fly, you must fly. If you were created to sing, you must sing. If you have a calling to write, you must write. We were all created to be free, so we must all be free.

We must be free to do things that matter most, or we will suffer. We must be free of injustice. We must be free of ridicule and prejudice that threaten to suffocate us. When you feel trapped, the instinct is to fight or escape and at times you freeze. You freeze because the sensation of heaviness is so overwhelming that you forget to breathe, and your entire body grows numb. It is only the deeper life within you that persuades you to survive. With every breath, the numbness begins to subside until you can take one step, then another, then another.

Nurturing the deeper life within you

You must nurture that deeper life within you in order to free yourself from the circumstances that threaten to tear you apart—chronic pain, loss, injustice. At times we engage and fight, but it can be exhausting having to fight the same battle over and over. Some situations call for cleverness where you have to find an alternate route and clear a different path. You learn to say *No more* when a conflict is too consuming. It does not mean that you were not a formidable opponent; it just means that you were wise enough to preserve and redirect your energies.

We nurture the deeper life within us when we decide to listen to the quiet within us. We listen to hear our innermost truths. We listen to receive the guidance that leads us in the direction of our next step. We become proficient at trusting our inner guidance system. The more we trust, the more reliable it becomes.

Ease does not mean lacking effort

Ease requires commitment and planning. It means you go about your day being intentional about maintaining a sense of balance. You do what usually works for you, discerning the best actions to take, deciding how and when, while remaining open to other options. Procrastination is not a valid option because ease is not stagnant. Instead, you prepare for the unexpected, allowing additional time when possible, recognizing that things do not always go as planned. Ease creates flow and movement, less resistance and less pressure.

Transcending Enslavement

Harriet Tubman *(c. 1820 ~ March 10, 1913)* said "I freed a thousand slaves. I could have freed a thousand more if only they knew they were slaves." These words resonate because we do not always recognize the things that bind and obstruct the free expression of all that we are. Shame, frustration, resentment, grudges—these are some of the emotions that keep us in a more contracted state and prevent us from embracing a greater sense of aliveness. Emotions exist so we can pay closer attention to how we are leading our lives and living our relationships. The energy of our emotions felt within our body can serve to direct our behaviors. Still, emotions are not designed to cause suffering.

Releasing shame and guilt

Shame, for example, leads to disconnection, self-loathing and other self-destructive behaviors. If you are feeling ashamed about your past, acknowledge and process those specific feelings. *Why am I still carrying around this emotional weight? How are these feelings serving me?* It is often the experience that we are most ashamed of that has the potential to empower us and allow us to be a source of encouragement to others. Dutch theologian Henri Nouwen *(January 24, 1932 ~ September 21, 1996)* offers that "when our wounds cease to be a source of shame, they become a source of healing."

Feelings of guilt typically indicate when you are out of integrity with yourself. Something you said or did might have caused harm. Instead of attempting to rationalize your words or actions, find a way to make amends or commit to doing better by replacing negative thoughts, patterns and behaviors with more affirming ones. Some of us also experience guilt concerning things that were beyond our control. How do we atone for the horrifying acts of some of our ancestors? The only way I can think of is to live our own lives with integrity, intention and purpose from this day forward, being mindful of the words of Saint Augustine *(November 13, 354 A.D. ~ August 28, 430 A.D.)*, "Charity is no substitute for justice…" Feelings of guilt do not right any wrongs. Instead, we must resolve to do no additional harm, seek fairness in all things and stand for what is right, not as an obligatory custom, but as a virtuous certitude.

Releasing blame

Blame only serves to reinforce the walls of the cage that we find ourselves in. If we place blame solely on our governing officials, then the power to effect change lies only with them. If we view our continued circumstances as *sins* of our parents, we comply with the perceived limits that have been set for us instead of rising beyond them. Or we might rise above those limits and still feel resentment, which only steals our joy. Instead, we must seek to heal from the wounds of the past, grieving the loss of innocence, unrealized potential and any other misfortune. We must grieve appropriately. We must surround ourselves with those who can truly understand our experience. We must find ways to replace unrealized hopes and dreams with new ones, from this day forward.

Learning to release blame is not about denying the reality of our circumstances; it is about recognizing that when we assume full responsibility for our lives, we can become empowered and more resourceful. If you had to delay educational pursuits due to a lack of financial means, recognize that nontraditional educational routes are still possible. Understand that even the most astute teenager can become addicted to opioids that were prescribed after an unexpected injury. Yet with guidance from parents and nonjudgmental support from their community, they too can overcome this unfortunate circumstance.

A life well-lived requires that we seek out opportunities that make a difference in our own lives and in the lives of others. Releasing blame says, *I will not let the misfortunes of my past determine my future wealth. I will not allow past hurt to steal present joy.*

Practicing detachment

There was a time when the word 'detachment' did not quite resonate. For me, it held the same frequency as disengaged or indifference. I now experience it differently in my body. It feels more freeing, much like surrender, as I no longer desire to have a firm grip on any one outcome. We cannot detach when we affix success to one specific result. I have learned to set my intentions, take whatever actions I can, and then I detach. I allow for possibilities I have yet to consider. I allow for further guidance. I practice patience. I remain hopeful.

~ PRACTICE ~

Paying attention to the messages of the body

Go out in nature and let yourself be drawn to an object you can hold in your hands. This might a twig, a rock, a flower, or anything else you can hold in your hand.

- First, spend time holding this object tightly. What do you experience in your body? What thoughts come to mind?
- Spend time holding the object loosely? Again, what do you feel?
- Now, hold on to this object in a way that feels most comfortable. Notice the response in your body.

The voice within says,

I flow easily with each experience that life offers to me. I see each challenge as another opportunity to learn and express something new. In peaceful surrender, I release destructive fears and doubts. I trust in the wisdom that created my inner being, body and mind. I trust in that same wisdom that created every other soul, body and mind.

Chapter 16

Abundance

Growing up I truly never considered my family to be poor. I believe this is because we had no insight into what other people had or did not have. Only close relatives entered someone else's home. We stayed outdoors to play. We drew Hopscotch squares in the dirt with a stick and marked our squares with pieces of glass. We played a game called rounders, only there was no bat just a ball we would throw in the air and hit with our other hand. There were always enough kids to mark the bases with our bodies. We had to reach and tag each *base* before we were tagged by someone from the other team holding the ball or before we were struck by the ball. We wore uniforms to school and none of us wore shoes except to church. When we were not in school, the ocean and *sea rocks* were our main playground. No one I knew under the age of ten owned a bathing suit.

"Why would anyone choose to be born into poverty," someone commented on a social media post. To which I responded, "…abundance is not just about material wealth. It is also about the abundance of compassion, love, hope, appreciation and trust that we come to embody as we navigate this existence…" This was a spiritual response because this post had appeared on Dr. Wayne Dyer's social media page.

From a practical standpoint, no parent envisions an impoverished life for their child. Most parents genuinely want their child's life to be better in all ways possible. It matters what we believe about our potential to transform our circumstances. If you tell a child that they can rise above their circumstances, they will believe you. If you set limits on their ability to succeed, they will likely aim for those limits and nothing further. We can either believe, "that poor kid doesn't stand a chance" or we can encourage that child's untapped potential by saying, "You did not have a fair start, but you still deserve every good thing that this life has to offer and you can create that for yourself."

"When you learn, teach"

I can now see how walking barefooted on the ground for many years led to a deeper connection to the earth. Not having electricity in my grandparents' home grew my love of storytelling. My uncles often had an entertaining story about their adventures at sea, fishing, diving and mishaps with recovering their lobster traps. Not having indoor plumbing nurtured my humility. I learned to cherish the sound of rain, especially as raindrops would strike the tin roof of our home, soothing me to sleep. Not having a television until we were much older allowed my trust to grow as I never knew the possible dangers of walking alone through what we called "the bushes." I imagine my grandmother's prayers followed me wherever I went. Not having a family car until I was about to graduate from high school allowed me to remain fit; we walked just about everywhere, only taking the public bus when necessary. I feel as though I am more appreciative of all that I have because I know what it means to have much less. I even have a greater appreciation for the ocean now because I see it less often.

Again, from a spiritual perspective, we come in with a circumstance, we learn the lessons we need and then we grow beyond our initial circumstances. Our lives are "the sum total of choices" as stated in the original post on Dr. Dyer's page that sparked the exchange about being born into poverty. Someone also questioned whether these were truly Wayne Dyer's words, which they were. They can be found in his book *Everyday Wisdom*.

We do not make the initial decisions that impact the earlier part of our lives. We cannot deny that there are some who commit the most terrifying acts against humanity. It is also a testament to the human spirit when someone overcomes the most horrific circumstances. In her book, *Led by Faith: Rising from the Ashes of the Rwandan Genocide*, Rwandan-American author Immaculée Ilibagiza tells her continuing story of being orphaned and alone after most of her family and friends were massacred. She had to rely on her abiding faith to guide and protect her in a world that appeared mostly bleak. She now shares her story of hope and faith to uplift others. "When you learn, teach…," Dr. Maya Angelou would encourage.

With love, all things are possible

Abundance is being aligned with love, recognizing that it is only through eyes of loving compassion that we often see our way past our inadequacies. Even the circumstances that threaten to limit our opportunities are often guideposts that point us in the direction of the real work we are meant to be doing in this world. In Chapter One I shared about the young woman who had been homeless from the age of eight until she was eighteen. She shared her appreciation for having a bed for the first time to call her own. She now desires to work with the homeless population, particularly children who are homeless.

No one chooses homelessness or poverty or tragedy to befall their lives. And yet, in any given situation, there is a choice between finding a way forward and giving up. There is a choice between aligning with love and being paralyzed by fear. There is a choice between staying in a place of continued suffering and helping someone else along the way. Redemption comes to those who believe it is possible. With love, all things are possible.

Being a rainbow in someone's cloud

> *"You may not control all the events that happen to you, but you can decide not to be reduced by them. Try to be a rainbow in someone's cloud,"*

~American poet and civil rights activist Dr. Maya Angelou

When I was young I overheard my mom one day, telling someone how she had found a fifty-dollar bill. She had been distraught about not having enough money to buy all the groceries we needed. She was on her way to the store and would have to decide between one necessity over another, but there it was, fifty dollars just lying on the ground before her. She made her way to the store and bought the groceries we needed. I must have been six years-old because my brother was able to stand, but still in his crib. I never forgot that story. I wonder if this planted a seed that my most urgent needs would be met.

I also remember the first time I lost something of great value. It was the first year of junior high school and it was a wristwatch with a leather band that was given to me by my parents. I remember trying to work up enough courage to tell them I had lost it, but I just couldn't. I feared being seen as careless. As I write this, I don't recall why I even felt the need to tell them since it belonged to me. I wonder if I just needed them to know how much it really meant to me and how horrible it felt to lose it. While I cannot recount the details that led me to the teacher who found it, I remember how grateful I felt when it was returned to me. There are people out there who will search for the rightful owner and return what is not theirs to keep.

And then there was a time in high school when I lost my wallet. At that time, I had been working at a store called Artland, folding T-shirts, so the money contained in this rainbow-colored wallet was money I had earned. I was more disappointed about the wallet than its contents. I can still remember its texture, plastic with swirls of raised painting. I also remember my hope that the person who found it was someone who could really use the money. I do believe that there are times when our small losses become someone else's blessings.

Transcending Unworthiness

You transcend unworthiness when you recognize that you are worthy and deserving simply because you exist. In the eyes of love, there is no need to earn your value. Each of us has inherent worth and yet we often measure this worth by the appreciation we are shown by the people in our lives. Maybe that wristwatch was a measure of how I believed my parents viewed me. In losing it, I felt undeserving of their trust. We lose things. We mess up. We make mistakes. We say the wrong things. The reality of this life is that we will not get everything right. We might unintentionally cause hurt to someone we care about. This is all a part of living this life. Mistakes are often how we learn. They do not make us less worthy. They make us human.

Our worth is not defined by the opinions of others. It comes from embracing all that we are, including the aspects of our selves that are not easily accepted by others. I can be Christian and still read and integrate other religious texts. I can practice my faith and still embrace the cultural dances of my Caribbean heritage that some might find indecent. I can read peer-reviewed journals and recognize that science does not have all the answers. I can possess fear and doubts and still live with authenticity and courage. I can be messy and creative, hopeful yet falter when the energy of the world's turmoil becomes overwhelming.

When he was Bishop of Geneva, Saint Francis de Sales *(August 21, 1567 ~ December 28, 1622)* is quoted as saying, "...For the love of God has been poured into our hearts by His Spirit dwelling in each one of us, calling us to a life of devotion and inviting us to bloom in the garden where He has planted and directed us to radiate the beauty and spread the fragrance of His Providence." I can feel the depth of these poignant words. I trust that you can too.

Some gardens need more tending to. We can bring in new soil and cultivate the terrain to make it more favorable. We can rely on more experienced *gardeners* to help us get started in planting the seeds for new hopes and dreams. We can recognize the unlimited wealth that is available to us when we release the struggle of holding on to former ways of being. We can clarify our priorities to determine what is non-negotiable. *What is within my power to change? What am I now willing to release that I chose not to before? Where can I seek the help that I truly need? If knowledge is power, how can I become more knowledgeable about this situation?*

Nothing leaves us…

Nothing leaves us before it teaches us what we need to know. I believe this to be one of the most difficult teachings to embrace; to do everything within one's power to overcome a persistent challenge, only to be faced with it again and again and again. For the longest while, I did not think the desire to mother another newborn would ever leave me. I now recognize that this long, winding road awakened in me a deep connection to and a respect for all of life, even in its earliest stages. I also understand that this is my journey and not the framework for anyone else's. If you don't share this belief, it is simply because this is not a significant part of your tapestry.

"We live and learn, or perhaps more importantly, we learn and live," said Sir Terence Pratchett OBE *(April 28, 1948 ~ March 12, 2015)*. We take what we learn and we apply it to the next adventure. We are never the same when we emerge from a challenging experience. Even when faced with a subsequent experience that might be similar, we are somewhat wiser, more compassionate and possess newfound strengths. This is life. Keep learning and growing. Keep leaning on the persons who show up at your side. Check in from time to time to be sure they are still solid enough to accompany you. If they can no longer be supportive, it just means you are meant to go the rest of the way without them, still never alone. "Your soul in its brightness and belonging connects you intimately with the rhythm of the universe," Irish poet John O'Donohue *(January 1, 1956 ~ January 4, 2008)* wrote in his book, *Anam Cara* which means "soul friend." Other people will appear as you need them if you allow them in. Still be discerning. If your focus is on being saved or on saving someone else, you are coming for a place of deficiency and most likely will attract someone lacking in solidity. If your focus is on learning to fish rather than being given one fish, you will create your own abundance.

Abundance is lightness

The feeling of abundance carries a sense of lightness rather than the heaviness that tends to weigh us down. For some, it is more freeing not to own a house. Instead, they move about, exploring different places, making a home wherever they happen to be for that period of time. Their greatest value is their freedom and so this is how they live abundantly.

Because of my roots, I have always chosen to live within my means. I admire clothing, but the brand makes no difference to me. I have had great finds at thrift stores even though I now have the means to shop elsewhere. For me, it is more about exploring things that were connected to someone else. I look at a piece of furniture and I see what images come to mind. *Who sat at this dining room table?* I touch something and I wonder *who wore this scarf before I did? Who did this butterfly brooch belong to?* Abundance is not solely about having money to spend, it is also being mindful of how our moments are spent.

~ PRACTICE ~

Planting Seeds of Abundance within Reach

One of the best ways to witness abundance is to grow something. It does not have to be an entire garden. You can regrow a head of lettuce from what is leftover at the base, just by placing it in water. It is extraordinary that water alone can allow for regrowth.

- Place a few inches of the base of the lettuce in a short glass with about half an inch of water. Place this near a source of light and observe what happens.
- Change out the water every other day. In about ten days to two weeks, you will notice sprouts.
- With the newly formed roots and leaves, you can then plant in soil so it can receive more nutrients. This can be done with celery, basil, green onion and other vegetables.

What have been some of your most abundant moments?

The voice within says,

I welcome opportunities to express my abundance. With every energizing breath, I feel gratitude for all that I am and all that I have lived. I am abundant in love and compassion, hope and trust.

Insight: Embracing Life, Discovering Beauty, Grace and True Purpose

Chapter 17

Courage

On August 1, 2019 as I began this chapter, images of an earlier time in my life (June 16, 2006) came to mind. This is what emerged.

A woman comes to the river's edge in search of solace. She has experienced a loss that could only be fully known to her. Like a broken promise, there is no visible wound. Yet the pain is immense, almost too much to bear. "Speak to me of courage," she queries through soft tears. "How do I do this…?

> *"My dear child,"* the voice of a departed one echoes. *"You are never to journey through pain and deep sadness alone.*
>
> *Cry out loud so that the winds of grace can hear your call for comfort.*
>
> *Stomp if you must, so that the ground beneath might rise to hold you if ever you should begin to fall.*

> *Just as these stones in and along this riverbed, allow the sorrows and the longings of your heart to mold and polish, but not destroy the essence of you."*

Pain, fatigue, loneliness, regret—do not allow any of these to cause you to hide away from life. Know that the courage to keep moving forward is held within the emptiness you now feel inside. Do not struggle to fill in this empty space. Do not attempt to bury it with busyness or excess. Instead, breathe deeply into the emptiness. Let this opening remain until it is ready to be filled. Be kind to yourself. Be patient with yourself for you have, within, all that you are in search of.

Exist more, not less

Do not mistake the adrenaline surging through your body, quickening your reactions, impairing your ability to make well-thought-out decisions for courage. Courage is not boisterous. It does not propel you into irreversible action. Yes, courage is bold. It emboldens you to be as you are, rather than conform. It permits you to question all that has been in order to discover what is most essential to all that you are. Allow this pain you now feel to carve a path to your innermost being. Here is where you will find all that you are seeking.

Courage is daring. It dares you to become all that you are capable of becoming, while allowing others to be as they are. You cannot expect anyone else to understand what you have lived. Neither is it your responsibility to change, convince or stand in judgment of others. Rather, it is to live your truth and share of your experience whatever you are called to share. Listen with respect when faced with a perspective that differs from your own. Hear what is true for them and know what is true for you.

While courage thrives with encouragement, it is not something to be found anywhere outside of oneself. Courage emerges from within so that you might exist more fully in the present world—so that you might help someone else to exist more fully.

Less space for shame and regret

As courage emerges, you are faced with a choice: Either to be shameful of your most vulnerable moments, regretful of what never came to be, or to live life from this moment forward. Your history, your family's history, even your nation's history—all of it has formed you into the person you are today with your beliefs, your principles, your values. Now, it is up to you to determine what beliefs may or may no longer serve your highest purpose. Which principles and values do you most want to live by? Do you live enslaved by shame, resentment or hatred? Or, do you recognize that your ancestry gave rise to your unshakeable faith and spirit of resilience? While you cannot change your past, there is an entire future awaiting your participation. What will you choose to create?

When there is less space occupied by shame and regret, you are better able to discern your highest needs. The courage within allows you to choose moments of solitude over isolation, patience with yourself over panic, integrity over powerlessness. It is through courage that you come to understand that grief is an ongoing process. You might think it is long past you, a childhood trauma, a distant loss, a haunting decision or lack of good judgment—and then, as unpredictable as an earthquake, you find yourself unbalanced again.

Forgive your past

Courage reminds you that forgiving your past will enable you to keep moving forward. It affirms that when grief resurfaces, it does mean it is here to stay. Acknowledge it. Give it space until it gives way to peace and calm. Seek support if this wave is too daunting to handle alone. If you speak out loud in the presence of someone who is mindful enough to listen, you will hear your innermost thoughts more clearly.

And when this grief recedes once more, notice who you are in this moment. Even if it stopped you in your tracks and appears to have set you back, you are still transformed beyond the person you used to be. Notice what has shifted within you. *What can you no longer deny? What are you most proud of within yourself? What are you most looking forward to?*

And what if this pain is unrelenting? What if chronic illness has you in a constant state of mourning for the healthier person you used to be? Allow this present version of yourself to grieve your former self without inner or outer criticism. Through grief, courage will bring you to acceptance—acceptance of your present life, your new reality, your less-abled body or less-abled mind. Reaching acceptance does not mean you will stay there, but the more times you return, the more habitual it becomes to let go of what you should or could have been. With courage you begin to recognize that this new way of being in the world does not change the essence of who you are, of who you have always been, of who you will always be.

Peace

Choose life

Courage says *do not wait until you are no longer afraid*. Make the choice to move ahead while being afraid. Choose hope when faced with uncertainty, perseverance when faced with pain, and self-acceptance when faced with intolerance—all while being afraid. If hope is met with disappointment, choose hope again and again and again. If pain is met with more pain, seek out other treatment options and continue to persevere, practicing self-care and surrender. And if self-acceptance is met with ridicule or prejudice, choose not to succumb to self-loathing. You free yourself from the bondage of other people's judgments and opinions by remaining true to the highest expression of your Self.

Courage beckons you to embrace life. Allow it to fortify you through times of grief, self-doubt and despair. Like an insightful director, the courage within holds the vision to transmute pain and grief into compassion, loneliness and self-doubt into self-discovery, and despair and confusion into hopefulness, discernment and clarity. Courage asserts that you choose life no matter how difficult it becomes or until it no longer becomes a choice. "Do not go gently into that good night," declared Welsh poet Dylan Thomas *(October 27, 1914 ~ November 9, 1953)*. Keep moving forward even if your hands shake and your heart races. No storm lasts forever, and you will experience peace once again.

Transcending Indifference

Grow into the fullness of all that you are, rather than disappear into the expectations of others. You may not have consciously chosen these circumstances, but this Life chose you as you are. There is no turning back as brother Khalil says of the river. It is not by chance who you are in this exact moment, in this chapter, in this ever-evolving story. It is not by accident where you live, your native language or your physical characteristics. Everything you are is what allows you to live all that has been placed within you. You must pursue your dreams even if no one else understands them. They are not meant to be understood by anyone else; they are to be fully lived by you.

> *It is said that before entering the sea,*
> *a river trembles with fear.*
>
> *She looks back at the path she has traveled,*
> *from the peaks of the mountains,*
> *the long winding road crossing forests and villages*
>
> *And in front of her,*
> *she sees an ocean so vast,*
> *that to enter*
> *there seems nothing more than to disappear forever.*
>
> *But there is no other way.*
> *The river cannot go back.*
> *Nobody can go back.*
> *To go back is impossible in existence.*
>
> *The river needs to take the risk*
> *of entering the ocean,*
> *because only then will fear disappear,*
> *because that is where the river will know*
> *it is not about disappearing into the ocean,*
> *but of becoming the ocean.*
>
> *~attributed to Khalil Gibran,*
> *author of* The Prophet

Finding 'Me'

And where does one find the courage to live their dreams? You must first come away from the river's edge. Be sure to plant your feet firmly on the ground. Now look inward, for I exist in you. I have always been here, providing guidance through an impelling urge or other bodily sensation, an intuition, a dream whose essence would not leave you until you paid closer attention. Get quiet and hear my voice more clearly. My voice, the voice of your innermost wisdom is a constant fount of inspiration. When you stop hearing me, become still and you will hear once again. Listen from the depths of your being, with your whole being.

> *"...You must distinguish My Voice from all the other voices...then you will be able to hold silent communion with Me at will, without interference from other's ideas, beliefs and opinions,"*
>
> ~The Impersonal Life, Joseph Benner,
> (1872-1938)

You will know my voice for it will not criticize or belittle. It will not place you in harm's way. It will not frighten you or magnify feelings of fear or insecurity. Instead, you will hear a voice of compassion, informing you from within, enabling you to feel more at ease, safe and secure. Listen for this voice whenever you feel unsettled, anxious or ungrounded. Be still and receive greater clarity. Be intentional and receive deeper insight. Be courageous in your search for me as I will also be seeking you.

And when you are ready, help others to turn inward and listen to the callings of their own fertile being. Lead them inward, but do not tell them what to see. They too have all that they need within them. Now go in peace for all is as it should be. *"All shall be well, and all shall be well, all manner of thing shall be well."* (Julian of Norwich, 1342-1416).

~ PRACTICE ~

Attuning to your innermost voice

- First, find a quiet, comfortable spot indoors or outdoors.
- Next, follow the steps as outlined in Chapter 5 to harmonize the body, mind and heart.
- Then, listen with your whole being; with your mind, your physical body, your emotional body, your innermost conscience, your deepest wisdom.
- What do you hear? What images come to mind?
- Write it down.
- Share it when you are ready

The voice within says,

I go within and explore the depths of my inner being. I remain open and receptive to the next steps that are illuminated along this path. I embrace the wisdom of my dreams and trust the guidance of my innermost voice.

Insight: Embracing Life, Discovering Beauty, Grace and True Purpose

Chapter 18

Emergence

How does a school of fish move as though there is one effective leader? Apparently, these synchronous movements are instinctual. According to Carnegie scientist Robert Hazen in a 2007 program by Nova scienceNow, "There is no leader. There is no director that's telling every fish where to go." Instead, by instinctively following three simple rules, namely; 1) stay aligned, 2) maintain a distance and 3) avoid predators, a collective intelligence naturally emerges. This applies to birds and bees, ants and even crowds of humans as they walk the city streets. What might appear to be random human behavior at first begins to form recognizable walking patterns and this happens subconsciously. Scientists refer to this phenomenon as *emergence*, where simple rules lead to complex patterns and behaviors that benefit the whole.

In this same program, another scientist, John Henry Holland (February 2, 1929 ~ August 9, 2015), explained that learning can emerge when a computer has been programmed to follow basic rules yet "the complexity of learning depends on how connected the parts are to each other." While a computer chip might hold billions of transistors, there are typically only three connections whereas the human brain with billions of neurons can have up to 10,000 connections. Billions of neurons with ten thousand individual connections allow for a complex operating system. "Some of us," Dr. Holland goes on to say, "believe that consciousness is the emergent phenomena of our brain connections."

The fabric we weave

Just this morning (July 11, 2020) I received a text message that reminded me of a dream I had back on April 18, 2020. In that dream, I was having a conversation concerning photographs that were in my phone's gallery. There were photos of a cardinal, a sea grape tree and one of a bridge in a rural setting. The bridge held my curiosity. It appeared to be an old footbridge across a narrow road with stone walls on either side. While still in my dream state, I realized I was no longer viewing the photo. Instead, it was as though I was standing alongside an empty, narrow road, looking upward at the bridge. No one else was in sight.

Soon after awakening that morning, I shared an actual photo of a cardinal from my phone with the person who had appeared in my dream. He once told me that the cardinal was one of his messengers so it made sense that he would be present in that dream. However, there were no photos of a bridge or a sea grape tree to be found. In his final message that day, my friend mentioned that he was supposed to have landed in Bermuda that afternoon had it not been for the pandemic.

The next day, I recalled the mention of Bermuda and felt compelled to search 'bridges in Bermuda' and then 'old bridges in Bermuda.' I looked through numerous images until I came across a photo that not only resembled the bridge from my dream, but also with the added details of a narrow road with stone walls. I would have been more stunned by this discovery had it not been for the prior experience I shared about in Chapter 7.

The person who had posted the photograph described the bridge as a "nice rustic old crosswalk bridge" with a caption that read, "A Road to Somewhere in Old Bermuda." Although he is a photographer, he indicated that this image was not his own, but had been taken by an unknown cameraman sometime in the early 1930's who had been part of an unknown group of tourists. The photograph was then processed and printed at a studio in Yokohama, Japan according to the additional details provided.

That day (April 19, 2020), I shared my dream with another friend, as well as the details that led to the discovery of the rustic bridge in Bermuda that resembled the one in my dream. Two days after, she sent me a text message that the island of Bermuda was to be featured that night (April 21, 2020) on the television show, *Chronicle*. We both decided we would tune in to see if the bridge would appear in the show. *How fun would that be.* Incidentally, she is the one who sent me a description of a sea grape tree that she happened to come across just last night (July 10, 2020), that sparked the memory of this dream. She had never heard of a sea grape tree before I shared about my dream and now three months later it comes up again, this time from a different source. From her message, I also learned something new. Apparently, the sea grape tree is also known in some places as an "autograph tree" where a passerby might write a message on its leathery leaves.

The exact footbridge was not shown on that episode of

Chronicle. However, there was a scene of a railway trail that matched the narrowness of the road in my dream with the stone walls along the sides. Coincidentally, the show also featured other photos by the same photographer responsible for posting the image of the footbridge in *Old Bermuda*. Had I not reached out to my friend who had appeared in my dream, I would not have learned of his intended trip to Bermuda nor would I have had any reason to look up bridges on that specific island. I had not seen or communicated with him since early March. I might have shared the dream with my other friend since we keep in touch more often, but there would not have been any reference to Bermuda and no reason for her to inform me of the episode on *Chronicle*. This is just one example of how our lives are so intertwined. One trivial piece of information connects with another and another.

Connectivity

The desire to feel more connected to something greater has led many of us to explore our ancestry through DNA analysis and research. At times it seems easier to connect to the past through something tangible. We all want to know where we came from especially during times when we have little to no idea of what could be next upon this grand adventure. While our past is important, we must also ensure our children's future. They are the "living messages we send to a time we will not see," said American author Neil Postman (March 8, 1931 ~ October 5, 2003). What do our children think about this time of unrest and polarization? Will they sing songs of oneness or will they walk to the beat of their own instrument, pursuing fame and avoiding any form of pain? Will continued protests change systems and give rise to leaders with integrity? What happens next? Are there other effective ways to engage in conversation so everyone can respectfully be heard? Will our children's children value a sense of real connection or will they seek comfort in simply fitting in? These are just a few of the questions for us to consider. Questions allow us to remain on the current path or consider more effective means to get us closer to where we would like to be.

Emergence is also defined as "the process of coming into view" or "coming into being." I think back to the image of the puzzle I share about in Chapter 6 where each person occupies a unique space that creates the space for someone else to exist as they are. We cannot predict how things will connect or how this continuing experience will unfold. Yet every person contributes to this process. How we think matters. Our beliefs matter. Our words, our choices, our decisions, how we interact with each other will determine what happens next. We do not have to share the same values and perspectives in order to appreciate our sense of connectivity. However, our future depends on our ability to connect deeply, communicate effectively and create new ways forward.

Transcending Disintegration

> *"...I see the world being slowly transformed into a wilderness, I hear the approaching thunder that, one day, will destroy us too, I feel the suffering of millions. And yet, when I look up at the sky, I somehow feel that everything will change for the better, that this cruelty too shall end, that peace and tranquility will return once more, in the meantime, I must*

hold on to my ideals."

~From the Diary of Anne Frank *(June 12, 1929 ~ February 1945)*

As I read these words by Anne Frank during this time, tearfulness arises. These are tears of deep understanding. I too have felt the suffering of others, the instability and extreme agitation of our time. And yet the reverence I have for this earth, our womb, grants me steadfast hope that peace and tranquility will return. I imagine many of you are hearing a similar call to remain anchored in hope and determine where you can best serve the integrity of the whole. Various scientists offer the perspective that at critical points of instability, something new emerges. I imagine that something new will soon emerge to benefit the collective, moving us into a state of greater congruence. There will always be conflict, but my hope is that we can become more adept at exchanging ideas and give birth to something more unifying.

What is your vision?

On the cover of the gift edition of Dr. Wayne Dyer's book, *The Power of Intention*, there is an image of what I once perceived to be one person with great strength holding up the entire world. This view likely originated from the Christian teachings, "He's got the whole world in his hands" and from various superhero themed movies. I now see this image differently. It is not up to one person or even one group to serve the needs of the entire world. It is up to all of us. Love-based interactions lean toward innovation and creative pursuits, while fear-based ones can be destructive. I now see this image as a person with outstretched arms welcoming a vision for a world he wishes to co-create. If more of us uphold a vision that is more harmonious, more just and more united, we honor the creative source from which we all emerged.

I believe Harriet Tubman said it best. "Every great dream begins with a dreamer. Always remember, you have within you the strength, the patience, and the passion to reach for the stars to change the world." The world changes not because of one singular action; rather, we sow seeds of change with each action. One action then leads to another and another and another. "We can do small things with great love," said Mother Teresa.

Begin where you are

Where to begin? This is often the question that keeps many of us at a standstill, not knowing which step to first take. The first step is to practice good self care so that you can serve from a place of wellness, not depletion. The basics are important; quality sleep and dream time, movement, proper nourishment and hydration, laughter and connection. And remember to b-r-e-a-t-h-e.

Then, start in your own home. What simple *rules* can your family follow that will allow for the best in all to emerge? The birds and the fish keep it simple; 1) Align, 2) Maintain good boundaries 3) Be aware. From there, look to your other relationships, your place of employment, your interactions with grocery store clerks, other drivers on the road. Recognize that every interaction is an opportunity to serve the good of humanity.

Spend time in silence, breathe deeply, commune with nature and explore your inner world, in solitude and in community. Consider keeping a journal as a helpful tool in identifying and acknowledging emotions of sadness, anger, guilt, resentment, frustration, numbness, fear, etc. Consider the positive aspects as well. Journals can hold joys alongside the tears. Share about grace and gratitude, affirming messages and insightful dreams. Think about something you wish to become more knowledgeable about. Educate yourself. Seek out groups and form meaningful relationships where you can speak your truth, sharing how you experience the happenings of this current world. Then, begin to think about the ways where you can best put your innate gifts to use.

In her *Ted Talk*, researcher Jane Adams invites us to consider how each person influences the happenings in our surrounding world. Rather than the "top-down power dynamics" we have become used to, how does one individual shape not only public policy, but also our evolution? Her questions caused me to ask similar questions. *What innermost value determines my vote, not just in a single election but wherever the opportunity presents to express the power of my perspective? How can my individual spending habits impact farming practices as well as market trends? How does my presence in a certain neighborhood, circle, or community contribute to its connectivity and wellness? How can I become a greater advocate for any person who is being abused, bullied or oppressed?*

My grandmother's message

In the past week, I have been visited by mourning doves. I was sitting on my deck when a lone dove came and landed nearby. It stayed quite a while, even allowing me to take a snapshot to share in my blog. Although supposedly widespread in this area, this was the first time I noticed one near our home. A few days later, while on the phone with my mom, I looked out the kitchen window and there were two doves sitting there. Almost exactly where I had seen one, there were now two.

Doves have been a sign of my grandmother's presence since her birthday in October 2012. One of my aunts had given me a candle holder that once belonged to my grandmother. It holds a statue of Christ at its center, with a dove on either side. One of the doves had been broken and what remains looks to me like a butterfly. *What do you think your grandmother's message is*, a friend asked about the recent visitation? When I messaged her about the doves, she shared that the home inspection company that had left her house moments before was named Dovetail Home Inspection. According to Collins English Dictionary, "if two things dovetail or if one thing dovetails with another, the two things fit together neatly…"

Now as I contemplate the appearance of the doves, these words arise from within me:

> *My dear, brokenness does not diminish wholeness.*
>
> *The dove is still a dove, though she now appears as the image of a butterfly.*
>
> *The butterfly is also whole as she is now; no mending required.*
>
> *See the beauty of the dove. See the beauty of the butterfly.*
>
> *Wherever she goes, whatever she*

> *becomes next, her essence will always be wholeness. See her in all her beauty.*

I now understand what Heraclitus meant when he proclaimed that *living and dying, waking and sleep, young and aged* are all the same. They are aspects of the same thing, not separate realities. Love and fear, hope and despair, joy and sorrow—all are integral to this human experience and the cycles we endure. Wholeness does not mean that we are never broken. To be human is to be vulnerable and still embrace all that this life has to offer. Beauty and grace will always be present along the trails, awaiting each of us to discover pieces for ourselves. How do we put it all together—well that is up to all of us as we reveal our treasures to each other.

This is my grandmother's most recent message to me, which I now share with you. That is true purpose. To live it, embrace it fully, then share it with others.

Gratitude

In my early years I did not possess many beautiful things, so it became easier to recognize the grace and just be thankful for the things I did have. While gratitude opened me up to the abundance that I now enjoy, it took growth and healing to be able to see the beauty amidst pain and uncertainty. I now recognize that by living fully and embracing all aspects of myself and this journey, I can share more deeply the gift of myself with others. It is not necessarily what I do but all that I have become in the process. This is the gift we give to each other—the gift of ourselves.

Peace

    An unfolding mystery is how I would best describe the process of writing this book and the connections I noticed along the way. I am grateful for the creative genius or geniuses that provided the inspiration and guided me through. Today's date is July 26, 2020 and I was curious to know which ancestors might have been born into this world on this day in history. I did a search and of course, I was immediately drawn to Swiss psychoanalyst Carl Jung (July 26, 1875 ~ June 6, 1961). He was the one to coin the term 'synchronicity,' defined as "meaningful coincidences." I feel immense gratitude for the seemingly unrelated occurrences that set me onto this path. Thank you for investing your time in reading what I have shared among these pages. I hope you find the practices and affirmations to be useful. May peace be with us all.

~ PRACTICE ~

Returning to Peace

Although this is the final practice, my hope is that it represents a new beginning for some of you. *Peace and harmony begin with self-knowledge.* I recently re-read this notation in my "Who Am I" workshop notes from April 4, 2008. What I did not recall was the cover image of these notes that was chosen by our PRH Educator, an incredible friend and teacher, Irma Gendreau. It was a photograph of a Great Blue Heron with the caption that reads, "Get to know the real you, not just an image of you!" I could not have made this up even if I tried, and yet my inner wisdom says, *we are all making this up as we go along.*

It is important that we become aware of our conditioned responses. This allows us to see the reality of ourselves and all that we experience more clearly, leaving space for the emergence of greater insight.

Be prepared to write in this practice and discuss with a trusted friend or within a healing circle. Remember this is not a once and done practice. It does not have to be completed in one sitting. Honor the process. Honor all that you are and all that you become.

1. As always, find a comfortable position and bring your awareness to your breath. As you breathe, become aware of all areas of your

body, any tensions, or any sensations. After a few deep breaths, rest your awareness in your heart.
2. When you feel ready, begin to consider how you see yourself.
    - Do I see myself in a mostly positive or negative way?
    - Does this change according to who I am with or dependent on a given situation? See yourself with different people.
    - How has my self-image changed throughout my life?
    - What remains my greatest challenge?
3. Now, consider how the people in your life see you?
    - What are some of the affirming messages I have received from others?
    - What are some of the negative messages I have received?
    - Which of these messages are mostly true and why?
    - What decisions have you made that you are most proud of?
4. Now, consider how you see the world around you, the people in your life, the places you feel most comfortable, and the activities you engage in.
    - With whom do I feel most at ease? Where do I feel safe and most comfortable?
    - What are some of the biases I hold about age, gender, race, ethnicity, social status, mental health, physical health? Where did they originate? How do these biases impact my interactions?
    - How do I engage with people whose perspectives differ from my own? How do I feel after these interactions? Is this how I wish to feel?
5. What intuitions have emerged from this process?

- Areas in my life in need of healing work, guidance or support?
- Any practices I would like to commit to?
- Simple changes I can easily make? Other changes that might take more time?

The voice within says,

I am Life's message of love, reverence and steadfast hope. I contribute to the harmony and wholeness of this beautiful and mysterious planet. I delight in all its wonders. I delight in all its beauty.

Kathleen Webster O'Malley

4 Simple Practices for Self-Healing

**The following practices are not a substitute to professional guidance or medical care. These are some of my favorite self-healing tools that many others have also found to be helpful.

1. **Practice Self-Compassion:** One of the best ways to deal with any form of adversity, insecurity or self-doubt is to be compassionate with yourself. A 2012 study in Clinical Psychology Review showed a decrease in stress, anxiety and depression in people who practiced self-compassion.

2. **Frontal-occipital holding:**
   Sends a calming response through your body.
   - This can be done seated or lying down.
   - Gently place one hand across your forehead.
   - Gently place the other hand on the lowest part of the back of your head.
   - Hold this position, while focusing on what is causing you discomfort,
     pain or anxiety or allow your mind to wander.
   - Deepen the relaxation response with slow, deep breaths, allowing your belly to expand with each inhale. (Hold

this position for 2-4 minutes)

3. Body Balancing Posture:
Restores balance and overall sense of calm.

- This can be done seated or standing.
- Cross your feet at the ankles, right foot in front of the left.
- Extend your arms out in front of you, then cross your right arm on top so that your palms can meet.
- Interlace your fingers.
- With your fingers interlaced, fold your arms downward and inward, resting your pinky fingers right at your chest.
- Place the tip of your tongue at the back of your front teeth.
- Now breathe. Breathe in for a count of 4, hold your breath for a count of 4, and exhale for a count of 4. (Repeat)
- Uncross your feet, then cross again at the ankles with the left foot in front.
- Extend your arms and cross your left arm on top, allowing your palms to meet.
- Interlace your fingers.
- Fold your arms downward and inward, resting your pinky fingers at your chest.
- Place the tip of your tongue at the back of your front

teeth.
- Again breathe. Breathe in for a count of 4, hold your breath for a count of 4, and exhale for a count of 4.
- (Repeat).
- (Repeat as needed).

4. **Practice Surrender:** We came into this world with nothing except that we were granted the ability to create amazing things, build incredible relationships, and leave behind love, hopefulness and other treasures that are enduring. Everything is a practice. Let us worry less about getting it right, enjoy the beauty of each moment, doing whatever we can and surrendering the rest.

Insight: Embracing Life, Discovering Beauty, Grace and True Purpose

Acknowledgments

While a book is mainly transcribed in solitude, it is never birthed alone…

I am grateful to my husband and daughter. Thank you for the space that allowed for seemingly endless hours of writing. Thank you both for your wit and humor. Thank you for your reminders to laugh and simply have fun.

Thank you to the Hay House Writer's Community under the guidance of Kelly Notaras, Founder and CEO of kn literay arts and Reid Tracy, President and CEO of Hay House Inc. Thank you for your enthusiasm and encouragement, generously sharing your expertise and providing a wealth of knowledge on all aspects of the writing, publishing, and promoting process. Thank you for inspiring the confidence needed to get this and other messages out into the world. Thank you to the members who connect, support and share in this uplifting community. (writerscommunity@hayhouse.com)

Thank you to Krista's family for allowing me to reveal how her life intersected with mine. She will always occupy a space in my heart.

Thank you to Gail Van Kleeck for your accompaniment in the writing process and for your keen eye for beauty and grace. Thank you for a nurturing writing space and for being an affirming presence. (gailvankleeck.com)

Thank you to Zorina Frey, Founder of I.W.A Publications and 45 Magazine Journal for your commitment to providing this platform and for your publishing expertise. Thank you for creating a local Literary Arts Open Mic that connected so many artists and visionaries. (iwapublications.com) (45magazineiwa.com)

Thank you to Raymundo Romero for a beautiful cover design that compliments my message of perseverance, grace and beauty. (raymundoromero.com)

Thank you to my PRH educators, Irma Gendreau and Mark Mariner (markmariner.com) who have supported my healing journey. Much gratitude to the members of my PRH family especially, Christine, Marie and Norman and my original FRA group, Cathy, Doris, Sarah and Eric. (prh-usa.org) (prh-international.org)

Thank you to Marcia Mariner for the *stone* you once gave to me and the guidance you provided. (marciamariner.com)

Thank you to Dr. Judith Swack for your trainings in Healing from the Body Level Up (HBLU) and your contributions to the field of Energy Psychology. (hblu.org) (hblutraining.com)

Thank you to Dr. Tisha M. Romero for your healing wisdom, love and support. Thank you for living this extraordinary experience alongside me though we are now miles apart.

Thank you to my Circle of Sisters for sharing your stories and sharing in mine. Thank you to Bernadette for bringing us all together with your heart-centered approach and sense of humor.

Thank you to the young women I met through Grafton Job Corps who have inspired me with your stories of resilience and expanded my view of how to exist in our world.

Thank you to Reverend Daniel Gregoire of the Unitarian Universalist Society of Upton and Grafton (UUSGU). Thank you for your encouragement and for being a source of much inspiration. Thank you also to the members of this incredible open-hearted community where all are welcome, no exceptions. (revdanielgregoire.com)

Thank you to Caroline Zani for creating a circle where we can gather and share about our mystical experiences. Thank you to Tina, Fran, Wendy, Tina who celebrates her birthday the entire month of April, Melissa, Lyv, Lisa, Mary, Anita, Eileen and the others who came from time to time. Some of your names escape me, but your essence will always remain. Thank you for sharing in this mystery. (carolinezani.com)

Thank you to all healthcare care workers and every person who serves in any capacity in a hospital or other healthcare facility. Thank you to that stranger in the ICU who told me I would be okay. You were right. I am.

Eternal gratitude to my grandparents, Virginia and Joseph Webster. Thank you for all that you lived, allowing me to exist as I am. Thank you for visiting me in my dreams and for your continued guidance.

My deepest gratitude to Dr. Wayne Dyer for lighting the way for this book to emerge. Thank you for your divine wisdom and continued inspiration. I imagine you are writing many more books from where you are. I will remain open. (drwaynedyer.com)

Much love and gratitude to my family, both near and far, and my friends too numerous to name here. Thank you for listening to my dreams and sharing about your experiences. Thank you to those who accompanied me on walks in nature, especially to one of my *special* places. Thank you for loving me and encouraging me. I am who I am because you are who you are. Thank you for being. I love you, eternally.

I acknowledge all the ancestors and guides, known and unknown, seen and unseen. Thank you for your guidance, your wisdom, your love. Thank you for reminding me that I am connected to the Source of all-that-is that loved me and everyone else into existence. Thank you for holding my hand in yours.

And thank you to anyone and everyone who revere this planet as much as I do. Thank you for your efforts to bring more unity, more justice, more harmony and more light so together we can *"heal the world, make it a better place for you and for me and the entire human race."*

Suggested Reading

Introduction: Integrity, Intention, Purpose

1. Malidoma Patrice Somé, *The Healing Wisdom of Africa: Finding Life Purpose Through Nature, Ritual and Community* (Tarcher/Putnam, September 13, 1999)
2. Dr. Wayne Dyer, *The Power of Intention* (Hay House Inc., December 15, 2005).
3. Joseph Benner, *The Impersonal Life* originally published in 1914 (Devorss & Co, June 1, 1941).
4. Dr. Wayne W. Dyer, *Living an Inspired Life: Your Ultimate Calling* (Hay House Inc.; Reissue Edition, March 1, 2016).
5. Karen Noe, *We Consciousness: 33 Profound Truths for Inner and Outer Peace* (Hay House Inc., March 27, 2018).
6. Gail Van Kleeck, *How You See Anything is How You See Everything: A Treasury of Simple Wisdom* (Andrews McMeel Publishing; First Edition, August 1, 1999).
7. Joel S. Goldsmith, *A Parenthesis in Eternity: Living the Mystical Life* (Harper One, January 1, 1855).

Chapter 1: Lifeward

1. Kathleen O'Malley, DC, *Messages from Within: Finding Meaning in Your Life Experiences* (Balboa Press, February 3, 2012).
2. Louise Hay, *You Can Heal Your Life* (Hay House Inc.; 2nd Edition (January 1, 1984).

Chapter 2: Openness

1. Wayne W. Dyer, *You'll See It When You Believe It: The Way to Your Personal Transformation* (William Morrow Paperbacks; 1st Edition (August 21, 2001).
2. Kathleen O'Malley DC, *Messages from Children…and What They Can Teach Grown-Ups* (Balboa Press, April 23, 2013).
3. Helen Keller, *The Story of My Life: By Hellen Keller-Illustrated* (Independently Published, July 21, 2017).
4. Pierre Teilhard De Chardin, *Hymn of the Universe*, Copyright 1961 by Editions du Seuil (Harper & Row, Publishers; First American Ed. Edition (January 1, 1965).

Chapter 3: Vitality

1. Jamie Sams and David Carson, *Medicine Cards: The Discovery of Power through the Ways of Animals* (Bear & Company, 1988).
2. Anita Moorjani, *Dying to Be Me: My Journey from Cancer, to Near Death, to True Healing* (Hay House Inc. 1st Edition, September 1, 2014).
3. Max Planck, *Where is Science Going?* Copyright 1932 (Muriwai Books, June 28, 2017)
4. Alex Z. Moores, *Living in Water* (Alex Z. Moores and Ta-Dah Publishing, January 10, 2017).

Chapter 4: Essence

1. Amos N. Wilson, *The Psychology of Self-Hatred and Self-Defeat: Towards a Reclamation of the Afrikan Mind*

(AWIS: Afrikan World InfoSystems, January 1, 2020).
2. Carl Sagan, *Cosmos* (Carl Sagan Productions, Inc. 1st Edition, January 1, 2010).
3. Hildegard of Bingen, *Book of Divine Works: With Letters and Songs* (Bear & Co; Original ed. Edition, June 1, 1987).
4. Albert Schweitzer, *The Light Within Us* (May 7, 2019).

Chapter 5: Harmony

1. Kathleen Hurley, Theodore Dobson, *My Best Self: Using the Enneagram to Free the Soul* (Harper One; 1st Edition, May 14, 1993).
2. Gregg Braden, *Human by Design: From Evolution by Chance to Transformation by Choice* (Penguin Random House, January 1, 2017).

Chapter 6: Oneness

1. Jalal Al-Din Rumi, Coleman Barks, *The Essential Rumi, New Expanded Edition* (Harper One; Reprint Edition, May 28, 2004).

Chapter 7: Purpose

1. Joseph Benner, *Christ in You*, originally published in 1919 (Merchant Books, November 9, 2015).
2. Louise Hay, Cheryl Richardson, *You Can Create an Exceptional Life* (Hay House Inc., September 20, 2011).
3. Kahlil Gibran, *The Prophet (Knopf,* September 23, 1923).

Chapter 8: Expression

1. Julian of Norwich, *All Will Be Well: 30 Days with a Great Spiritual Teacher* (Ave Maria Press, Inc., March 15, 2008).
2. Julian of Norwich, *Revelations of Divine Love* (Digireads.com, January 1, 2013).
3. Caroline E. Zani, *Waiting for Grace* (Wyatt-MacKenzie Publishing, January 31, 2020).

Chapter 9: Genius

1. Elizabeth Gilbert, *Big Magic: Creative Living Beyond Fear* (Riverhead Books; Reprint Edition (September 27, 2016).
2. Matthew Walker PhD, *Why We Sleep: Unlocking the Power of Sleep and Dreams* (Scribner; Reprint Edition, June 19, 2018).

Chapter 10: Reverence

1. Alice Walker, *Her Blue Body Everything We Know: Earthling Poems 1965-1990 Complete* (Mariner Books; First Edition (May 19, 2003).

Chapter 11: Alignment

1. Gail Van Kleeck, *Simple Wisdom for Challenging Times: Revised Edition*

(Independently Published, August 11, 2019) originally published in 2004.

2. Kyle Gray, *Angel Numbers: The Message Behind 11:11 and*

Other Number Sequences (Hay House UK, November 19, 2019).

3. Ta-Nehisi Coates, *Between the World and Me* (One Word; 1st Edition, July 14, 2015)
4. Miguel Ruiz, *The Four Agreements: A Practical Guide to Personal Freedom (A Toltec Wisdom Book)* (Amber-Allen Publishing Incorporated, July 10, 2018).
5. Mattie J.T. Stepanek, *Reflections of a Peacemaker: A Portrait Through Heartsongs* (Andrews McMeel Publishing: 1st Edition (August 1, 2005).

Chapter 12: Creation

1. Howard Thurman, *Jesus and the Disinherited* (Beacon Press; Reprint Edition (November 30, 1996) originally published in 1949.
2. Rainer Maria Rilke, *Letters to a Young Poet* originally published in 1929 (Dover Publications, May 8, 2002).
3. Matthew Fox, *Original Blessing: A Primer in Creation Spirituality* (Bear & Company, 1983).

Chapter 13: Enduring

1. Howard Thurman, *Jesus and the Disinherited* (Beacon Press; Reprint Edition (November 30, 1996) originally published in 1949.
2. Judith Swack, PhD, *Healing from the Body Level Up 1* Training (Copyright HBLU, Inc.).

Chapter 14: Presence

1. Paramahansa Yogananda, *Autobiography of a Yogi* (Self-Realization Fellowship, January 5, 1998)
2. Bronnie Ware, *The Top Five Regrets of the Dying: A Life Transformed by the Dearly Departed* (Hay House Inc., August 13, 2019)
3. Serena Dyer, Dr. Wayne W. Dyer, *Don't Die with Your Music Still in You: My Experience Growing Up with Spiritual Parents* (Hay House, Inc. June 16, 2014).

Chapter 15: Ease

1. Henri J. Nouwen, *The Wounded Healer: Ministry in Contemporary Society* (Image Books Doubleday, February 2, 1979)

Chapter 16: Abundance

1. Dr. Wayne W. Dyer, *Everyday Wisdom* (Hay House Inc., February 1, 2005)
2. Immaculée Ilibagiza, *Led by Faith: Riding form the Ashes of the Rwandan Genocide* (Hay House; Original Edition, September 25, 2008)
3. John O'Donohue, *Anam Cara: A Book of Celtic Wisdom* (Harper Collins; 1st Edition, November 1, 1998)

Chapter 17: Courage

1. Joseph Benner, *The Impersonal Life* originally published in 1914 (Devorss & Co, June 1, 1941).
2. Julian of Norwich, *All Will Be Well: 30 Days with a Great*

Spiritual Teacher (Ave Maria Press, Inc., March 15, 2008).

Chapter 18: Emergence

1. Robert M. Hazen, *The Story of Earth; The First 4.5 Billion Years, from Stardust to Living Planet* (Penguin Press, July 30, 2013).
2. John H. Holland, *Emergence: From Chaos to Order* (Helix Books, April 23, 1999).
3. Anne Frank, *Anne Frank: The Diary of a Young Girl* (Bantum Reissue Edition, June 1, 1993).
4. Wayne W. Dyer, *The Power of Intention: Learning to Co-create Your World Your Way* Gift Edition (Hay House Inc.; Gift, Reissue Edition, October 1, 2010)

Acknowledgements:

1. Kelly Notaras, *The Book You Were Born to Write* (Hay House, Inc. November 13, 2018)
2. Gail Van Kleeck, *The Magical Interior Design: Ideas for Improving Your Inner Spaces from the Home Decorating Fairy Godmother* (Independently published, July 2, 2019)
3. Zorina Exie Frey, *45 Magazine Women's Literary Journal: A Story for Every Woman* (45magazineiwa.com)

Insight: Embracing Life, Discovering Beauty, Grace and True Purpose

About the Author

Kathleen Webster~O'Malley received her Doctor of Chiropractic degree in April 1999 as a graduate of New York Chiropractic College magna cum laude. She is an integrative wellness practitioner with an office in North Grafton, Massachusetts. Kathleen is also a prolific writer with the intention of sharing inspirational and transformational stories and messages. In addition to *Insight: Embracing Life, Discovering Beauty, Grace and True Purpose*, she is also the author of *Messages from Within: Finding Meaning in Your Life Experiences* in which she shares her personal story of healing and transformation. Her second book, *Messages from Children and What They Can Teach Grown-Ups* is about leading a more authentic, life-affirming existence. Kathleen has also served as a mentor to teens and young adults. She believes that we are ultimately called to serve in areas where we have experienced the most pain, allowing us to see the beauty and grace of our true connectedness in this intricate web of life.

You are invited to subscribe to her blog at

www.kathleenomalleymessages.com.

www.ingramcontent.com/pod-product-compliance
Lightning Source LLC
LaVergne TN
LVHW041612070426
835507LV00008B/203